# THE PFI/PPP AND PROPERTY
## A PRACTICAL GUIDE

by

MARTIN BLACKWELL

2002

A division of Reed Business Information
ESTATES GAZETTE
151 WARDOUR STREET, LONDON W1F 8BN

First published in 2000 by Chandos Publishing (Oxford) Limited
This reformatted edition published by Estates Gazette in September 2002

ISBN 0 7282 0391 X

© M. Blackwell, 2000

Printed in Great Britain

# Contents

## Appendices

# The Author

Martin Blackwell's professional career commenced at Prudential Portfolio Managers in London. He is presently Head of Property and PFI Consulting for Peterborough firm, Colin Brooks Associates. Martin Blackwell has a first class honours degree in Urban Estates Surveying from Nottingham and has received the Estates Gazette Award and Robert Clarke Prize. Martin has contributed to a number of journals on the subject of PFI, in particular the *Private Finance Initiative Journal*, and *Planning Magazine*, the journal of the RTPI. Martin has spoken at a number of national conferences on various aspects of PFI and PPP and also has considerable practical experience, having advised a number of consortia on bids as well as public sector side bodies such as Norfolk Constabulary. Martin is a member of the RICS PFI Policy Panel and was a contributor to the RICS PFI Guidance Notes.

The author can be contacted through the publishers.

# List of Abbreviations

| | |
|---|---|
| 4Ps | Public Private Partnerships Programme |
| ASB | Accounting Standards Board |
| BAFO | best and final offers |
| DETR | Department of the Environment Transport and the Regions |
| FEFC | Further Education Funding Council |
| FM | facilities management |
| FRS | Financial Reporting Statement |
| GDP | Gross Domestic Product |
| HEFC | Higher Education Funding Council |
| ISOP | invitation to submit outline proposals |
| ITN | invitation to negotiate |
| ITT | invitation to tender |
| MoD | Ministry of Defence |
| NHS | National Health Service |
| NPV | net present value |
| *OJEC* | *Official Journal of the European Communities* |
| PFI | Private Finance Initiative |
| PIM | pre-qualification information memorandum |
| PIN | prior information notice |
| PPP | Public Private Partnership |
| PSBR | Public Sector Borrowing Requirement |
| PSC | public sector comparator |
| PSP | private sector provider |
| RFQ | request for qualification |
| RICS | Royal Institution of Chartered Surveyors |
| TUPE | Transfer of Undertakings (Protection of Employment) Regulations 1981 |

## Chapter 1

# The PFI: an introduction to the history, the process and key terms

This work cannot hope to cover the entire field of PFI and PPP projects. The aim of the author is to provide a practical guide to projects having a substantial real estate element: in order that the professional members of the project team on either the client side or that of the bidder may readily comprehend key issues from a property perspective. One important defining aim of 'a practical guide' is to be of use to those using it. The author has therefore drawn on experience to offer suggestions as to how bid prospects may be improved. The guidance given should be invaluable to consortia, or component companies, which have yet to reach financial close on a range of projects. For those that have reached financial close and are versed in PFI procedures the book explores areas where affordability may be enhanced and value for money increased. (In certain areas of the public sector 'value for money' has more correctly become 'best value'.) Areas are also given over to discussing concepts like risk transfer together with other property-related issues.

The public sector manager faced with the need to explore PFI will find great benefit in the work as a starting point in understanding the process. A range of examples and issues are discussed from the public sector viewpoint. It is hoped in conclusion to draw the public and private sectors together with a more complete understanding of the issues faced in PFI and PPP projects.

## PFI – an introduction

In simple terms the Private Finance Initiative, launched in 1992 under the last Conservative administration, had as its main tenet the involvement of the private sector more directly in initial asset provision and the subsequent operation of the service. The aim was to deliver higher quality more cost-effective public services.

On taking office in May 1997 the Labour administration launched a review of the PFI known as 'The Bates Review'.[1] The Bates Review made 29 recommendations designed to streamline the PFI process. This in itself gives some idea of the underlying complexity present within the PFI process prior to the review, and although matters have improved the PFI process is not without its complications and jargon. This chapter attempts to provide a logical understanding in the clearest possible fashion.

Since the initial Bates Review a number of PFI principles have become more clearly established. However, Sir Malcom Bates has been tasked with a second review, while a whole range of organisations from the European Parliament to the Accounting Standards Board have affected the process. A number of the issues raised by these bodies have become mainstream media news. The more important of these will be considered later, not in a historical or theoretical context, but in relation to practical issues raised.

The attitude of the Labour administration to the PFI provides evidence that the Initiative is here to stay. Changes may be made to the detail of the approach and it seems likely that increasing use will be made of the phrase 'Public/Private Partnership' rather than PFI. However, there is mainstream cross-party recognition that private funds are required for certain public works.

In a pure sense there is a range of conditions which need to be met in order for a PFI project to occur, and a Public/Private Partnership will also need to meet the legal requirements set out for such arrangements. However, the process is less involved than with a pure PFI scheme. There is likely to be increasing use of both expressions in a political context to the extent that they may become interchangeable, though they are not strictly interchangeable at present.

The economic driver for an approach at least akin to the PFI is the stated aim of reducing the Public Sector Borrowing Requirement. If the public sector does not possess the money to invest in the capital creation of projects then this must come from the private sector.

Why is the government making the private sector borrow the money to finance these projects when the public sector can borrow the same money at a cheaper rate? The answer lies in the belief that the private sector can introduce cost savings and efficiency gains to a project. Government has set out this view in a worked example in *The Private Finance Initiative. The Government's Response to the 6th Report.*[2] The argument is that over the life of a typical PFI project the costs could be apportioned roughly as 30 per cent for the capital (construction) element and 70 per cent for the operational element.

Government experience of contracting out services under the Competing for Quality programme suggests private sector efficiency gains of 20 per cent. This would translate into savings for the operational element of PFI deals of 14 per cent (ie a saving of 20 per cent on 70 per cent of the cost). In respect of the construction element past experience of publicly funded construction projects shows an average of 24 per cent cost overruns, a risk which under the PFI would be borne by the private sector. Assuming the private sector is better able to manage these risks, the saving on the capital element could be up to 7 per cent (ie the 30 per cent construction element with a saving of 24 per cent). In respect of the cost of finance the government has estimated that the cost to the private sector may be 3 per cent higher. If construction and operational savings are achieved, a 17 per cent better value for money project would still result when compared to the public sector alternative.

The above is not without its critics, though it does illustrate why PFI may be attractive. However, the numbers are rather broad-brush and global. The calculation fails to factor in differences between projects in different sectors and projects of different sizes. In looking at a PFI project it should not be assumed that it is going to be 17 per cent cheaper than the public sector alternative. Many smaller projects, with which smaller organisations have become involved, have been expensive. The procurement process has been long and costly and due diligence required by funding banks has further increased the expense.

The PFI came about as a means of increasing capital and service provision in an economic environment pressured by tight spending controls. The financing of public sector capital spending was originally charged to the PSBR in one year. In order to reduce the PSBR one of the early attractions of the PFI was the ability to have transactions which remained off balance sheet. By financing payments for usage over a period of time rather than the original capital cost the government could achieve more in terms of the number of projects and the amount of service provision.

The government dealt with the issue of the cost of borrowing by reflecting on private sector efficiency savings and initiative. The 'initiative' leads to the importance of alternative revenue streams and similar concepts within the PFI process. Whether the private sector is more efficient, cost savings actually occur and service provision is enhanced will depend on the findings of the Audit Commission and others – not now, but after a number of contracts have completed a substantial period of the operational phase.

In a PFI scheme the successful bidder constructs the necessary output, maintaining it and providing an agreed service level for the duration of the contract. Over a typical contract term of 25–30 years it is not the capital cost of the construction which is the most important variable but the cost of providing the ongoing service. In a typical property based project it has been calculated that approximately 75 per cent of the total lifetime cost relates to the service provision as opposed to the 25 per cent which relates to the construction.

Many in the public sector have a project which they wish to get off the ground. All they need is someone to build it for them. The ongoing costs can probably be supported but not the initial capital expenditure. Will the PFI supply the answer in the shape of the necessary capital funding? From the viewpoint of the public sector manager this is probably the key question. It has also led the government to seek to prioritise projects and to introduce regulations and processes of approval in each area of public sector activity.

The regime is different for both local authority and central government projects. Projects in the health sector may need national sanction or, if they are below a specified level, Regional Health Authority approval. The education sector again operates in a slightly different manner. For the present we can ignore some of these differences: the public sector body will need to be aware of the process by which a project is to be sanctioned; the private sector should seek evidence that such sanction has been obtained. If the sanction has not been obtained the project cannot progress and the private sector will be engaged in an expensive process which can go nowhere. While differing regulations may seem to complicate the process, the basic concepts are the same, and these are explored in this book. Sectoral differences will be commented upon to illustrate practical points. The key at this stage is for the public sector manager to recognise that there will be a set of rules with which compliance will be required while the private sector should not hesitate in asking to see evidence of compliance with the sanctioning process.

## The PFI process – receiving central government endorsement for local authority projects

The Project Review Group, a body established by the government, has the task of endorsing all local authority PFI projects that require revenue support prior to the procurement process commencing. The process between project identification and procurement for a local authority project is as follows:

1   Identify the need for the project and justify the business need.
2   Consider the funding options available.
3   Establish the necessary level of support from elected members or others.
4   Will PFI be likely to deliver 'value for money' or 'best value'?
5   Appoint professional advisers and take advice on the scheme.
6   Discuss the project with the relevant government department and representatives, the 4Ps or others established with this role. (The 4Ps refer to the Public Private Partnerships Programme, which seeks to promote the use of the PFI.)
7   Draft the outline business case with the input of the advisers, particularly the financial, property and technical advisers.
8   Secure commitment from elected members or decision-makers.
9   Submit the project to the relevant government department.
10  The government will consider the project against criteria (due to the need for revenue support).
11  If the department endorses the project it will be submitted to the Project Review Group.
12  The Treasury Taskforce (or other body with this function) will scrutinise the project.
13  The Project Review Group will endorse the project.
14  Following endorsement procurement may commence with a notice in the *Official Journal of the European Communities (OJEC)*.

The above project approval process may be used as a template for projects in all sectors where the decision of the public sector body to enter into a scheme needs to be considered by others. For example, with a small-scale health sector scheme the Regional Health Authority may take on the role of the government department and project scrutiniser.

Some local authority schemes have been self-financing, eg a car parking scheme in Guildford. Such schemes do not require revenue support and the sanctioning process is dramatically reduced. The fact that some schemes can be self-financing while others require revenue support illustrates the commercial world in which PFI and PPP projects operate. The finance will need to come from somewhere. If the project is financially viable without a grant or financial support, the public sector body has an attractive proposition for which private sector interest is likely to be high.

Rather akin to a city centre redevelopment site with retail planning permission, it is not a question of finding a development partner, but choosing which one. If revenue support is required it is a question of putting forward the best business case possible, as those seeking support are in direct competition with others seeking funds from that allocation.

Any revenue support received from central government is not intended to cover the whole of the annual charge to the PFI contractor. The revenue support is aimed at covering that part of the annual charge, which relates to the financing of new capital investment. The total cost of the contract is abated by an amount which relates to that part of the contract that is assumed to relate to ongoing services. Local authorities already receive revenue support for these items.

The better the business case and the more financially viable the project, the greater the prospects for completion. If revenue support is required it would be advisable to bid sooner rather than later: the logic of the process has yet to catch up with what will happen in ten years' time when annual revenue obligations then occurring exceed that which is comfortable.

Understanding the PFI process is critical to success in the PFI field. Until the time of the *OJEC* Notice it is likely to have been the public sector body which will have been attempting to jump hurdles in order to get the project approved. Following the *OJEC* Notice the private sector should appreciate that what they are trying to do is also jump hurdles: they are trying to pass the selection threshold at each point in the PFI process. Much of the focus of this book is aimed at improving the prospects of a bidder passing each stage until the position of being preferred bidder is reached.

Following the *OJEC* Notice the public sector body will evaluate all responses and create either a long or short list. If a long list approach is followed it will merely add another stage to reduce the number of interested parties from about seven or eight to four or five. The additional stage will allow for the asking of more involved questions in order to aid the evaluation process.

When a short list stage has been reached the invitation to negotiate (ITN) will be issued to those parties that remain. Responses to the ITN will be received and analysed. It is likely that bidders will have the opportunity to present the ITN response to the decision-making executive of the public sector body.

A request for best and final offers (BAFO stage) may follow the ITN. A preferred bidder will be selected from BAFO evaluation with a reserve bidder also likely to be nominated. From experience it is strongly recommended from the public sector viewpoint that some competition be retained in the process for as long as possible.

Following the selection of the preferred bidder final detailed negotiations will take place and the contract will be signed. The point of financial close will have been reached. At this stage the work should be that of fine-tuning the agreement, akin to completing a contract on agreed and detailed heads of terms. Unfortunately this is not always the case and reaching final close can be a drawn-out process. This may be due to the bidder trying to renegotiate; alternatively the public sector client may be seeking to alter the scope of the work. The professionals involved in the process will have an important role to play. Chartered surveyors have not been recognised to date as being amongst the key lead advisers – accountants and solicitors are usually identified with such prominence and have high fee accounts. The technical advisers are identified with much lower fee bills, and less of a role in the conclusion of the deal. However, the skills of a surveyor suitably experienced in PFI in drawing the parties together before and after preferred bidder selection should not be underestimated. Property professionals are accustomed to bringing developers and contractors together and have an understanding of the process.

A good lawyer will of course be necessary on either side of contract completion. It is, however, important to be able to put the legal issues arising into context. This is where the experience and acumen of the lawyer will be important. A PFI contract actually involves many subcontracts, which will need to take an acceptable form for both parties. The devil may be in the detail, yet some of the detail needs to be put in its place. Ask the question, 'is a particular issue a deal breaker or not?' A good lawyer will know, a poor or inexperienced one will not.

Accountants have acquired prominence in the PFI process under the title of financial advisers. A myth has been created around the 'financial model', the tool by which bids at later stages in the process are judged. The bids are compared with each other and other options, for example the public sector comparator. Control of the financial model has given the accountant an important role in the process, and he or she perhaps more than the lawyer or the technical adviser will have the single greatest impact on who is selected as preferred bidder. In many bidding consortia the financial advice may be kept in house although the public sector is likely to appoint an external financial adviser. The financial adviser appointed by the public sector should be capable of liaising with that body's auditors throughout the process. A number of accountancy treatment issues will be raised which both the public sector and the bidder will have to address. Unfortunately, accountancy treatment is one of those areas which has impacted negatively, and in many ways illogically, on the PFI process.

Having read the above one may ask why PFI is worth considering by the contractor. Does it not involve a lot of time, effort and money for an uncertain return? The answer is that it may, yet the PFI and PPP are becoming established and serious operators will need to identify and research sub-markets in which they feel comfortable to operate. One point to be stressed is that, despite the process and the accountancy profession's standardisation of many risks, PFI projects in different sectors are not the same. Clients in certain sectors should expect a higher return than in others, while the actual construction, operational and property risks should be viewed differently too. Part of the PFI learning curve is to establish ground rules for the type of project you will consider. Do not view the PFI as simply another way to win a building contract – it can be more than that, and to maximise your return it should be.

## Why is PFI worth considering by the contractor?

One of the first sectors to pour scorn on the PFI was the construction sector. As it was the construction sector which had provided buildings under traditional procurement arrangements it was naturally seen by many in the public sector as being the provider of buildings and services in a PFI contract. If the construction sector did not like the PFI, surely this was reason enough for the public sector not to like it. While much of the initial hostility of the construction sector has been overcome, concerns remain about the cost of the bidding process. There is anecdotal evidence that many (larger) players in the construction sector dismissed the PFI in public yet furthered such schemes privately, the public dismissal being an educated lobbying of government and an attempt to reduce the number of players in the market. Many construction companies have still to understand the PFI process and the impact it will have on their core business.

Construction has traditionally been cyclical, with the further burden of the low profit made as a percentage of turnover. The City doesn't like such business, despite arguments from contractors that the capital employed is low. The PFI and PPP provide the perfect opportunity to reduce the exposure of the business to market cycles as contracts to provide services may be for 30 years. Rather than the old position where the contractor builds and leaves, here is an opportunity to secure an income stream for 30 years through the provision of services (facilities management). Not only is the exposure to market cycles reduced but the capital employed in providing the services (which at present yields a greater profit) is little more than that necessary for the original construction.

The PFI can only be seen as a way to obtain a building contract if you are part of a larger group where another company is providing the facilities management services. If one consortium becomes preferred bidder and that consortium does not contain a contractor they may tender the building contract. You may source work in that way yet it will be competitive and you will still need an understanding of the PFI process in which you will find yourself operating.

One aim of this book is to attempt to aid organisations in bidding for projects. However, not all projects ought to be considered. Many smaller projects have suffered from high bid costs, which have also hindered the public sector. If the government wishes to expand the use of PFI or like-minded PPPschemes, the standardisation of legal templates and financial models is a must. The real winners from PFI to date have been a relatively small group of lawyers and accountancy-based management consultants. Those used to bidding for projects in the education sector have experience of putting numbers into an FEFC or HEFC standard model. No such template exists for bidders to PFI projects to gauge whether a bid ought to be made, and no such template exists to assist the public sector in considering the project viability.

## Private sector PFI-style arrangements

Some introductory mention needs also to be made of so-called private sector PFI-style arrangements. These have evolved as a way of removing certain types of property asset from the balance sheet. They may be suited to a number of circumstances where the property in question is very specialised. The essence of the contract is similar to a public/private PFI arrangement. One party designs, builds, finances and operates the structure; the other party makes a payment for occupation and usage. While the procurement process is different, much of the principal contract detail will be similar. There will be provisions to determine the amount and nature of the payment, to cover poor service performance and to address the ultimate ownership of the asset. Those considering involvement with a private sector PFI-style contract would benefit from seeking the advice of a party who has been involved in a standard PFI contract. Later sections of this book dealing with service provision will be of particular relevance.

## The key concepts within the PFI

The PFI process introduces a number of concepts upon which it is necessary to comment. Understanding the jargon is necessary on the bidder side to show an understanding of the process. Attend a briefing day and ask, 'what is risk transfer?' and the likelihood of your being shortlisted for the project will be slight if any of the client side project team can identify you.

A Glossary of PFI terms is provided in Appendix 2 at the end of the book. In order to be able to continue without interruption it may help some readers to consider the Glossary prior to reading further, although some terms are so fundamental to the PFI that they do need a text introduction. The following are key basic terms.

### The public sector comparator

All projects are to have a PSC which is used to measure the privately funded alternative in terms of offering value for money or best value. The nature of what the PSC is for a given project can provoke debate. The private sector would like to know the actual cost of the PSC in NPV (net present value) terms. The public sector may not wish to release the NPV, at least in the initial stages of bidder selection. In all cases the private sector should understand how the PSC has been calculated. The same factors should apply as with the PFI project in order to compare like with like. In certain cases the PSC may be notional – there might not actually be a publicly funded alternative capable of occurring.

### Value for money

In simple terms this occurs when the privately funded project has a lower NPV than the PSC. However, the NPV may not be the only factor of a financial nature which is considered; the actual timing of the payments over the contract period may impact on the public sector value for money equation. Best value is an extension and slight redefinition of the value for money concept. In theory best value may take a more holistic approach to the provision of groups of services.

## Affordability

The privately funded scheme has to be affordable. The NPV of the project may need to be below a given figure (and definitely the PSC, without good reason to depart from this); the payments under the contract must also be affordable. The private sector would wish to see an indication of the affordability threshold for a project. For the public sector this is akin to stating how much they have to spend. At some point in the bidder selection process affordability levels are likely to be clarified; this is unlikely to be at the start of the process.

## Single unitary charge

The private sector constructs the building and operates the service for which it is paid a single unitary charge, the theory being that the public sector should make just one payment for their occupation. Rating law has yet to fit in with government decrees on the single unitary charge and consequently the public sector body is likely to be paying the charge and business rates, which are a tax on the occupation of property. More comment is provided on property issues later in this work, of which this is one topic which is discussed.

## Alternative revenue streams

Ideas for third-party income can arise from the project or because of the project. The third-party income is likely to be split in an agreed fashion between the bidder and the public sector client. The client may benefit from these alternative revenue streams as they can be applied to reduce the single unitary charge and consequently make the project more affordable. If the bidder can assist in making the project more affordable and in reducing the single unitary charge he will be increasing dramatically the chances of his bid being successful.

## Risk transfer

For reasons which we shall explore later risk transfer needs to occur in PFI projects. The concept involves the passing of various risks from the public sector to the private sector. A degree of risk transfer will need to take place for a PFI project to occur. While there has been a tendency for the public sector to attempt to pass all the risks associated with the project to the private sector, the private sector will price all risks transferred and consequently transferring all risks may not offer the best value as the price is likely to increase. The concept of having the risks with the party best able to manage them has arisen.

### The bidder

The bidder is generally considered as the party bidding for a PFI contract. This may be one company or organisation or a grouping of a number of such bodies. Consortia are becoming increasingly common and links are being established between organisations to work on different types of project in different market sectors. The client is usually seen as the public sector body procuring the service.

## Chapter 2

# Property and PFI

The focus of this book is on the property and construction sectors and to those who work with them and advise them. It should be remembered that PFI and PPP projects exist in a wide range of sectors which have little to do with the built environment. Many information technology PFI schemes have been concluded without either the client or the bidder reflecting for more than a moment on property matters.

A great many PFI and PPP projects are, however, designed to procure an accommodation solution and service, or to procure a service which is heavily reliant on the need for real estate in its delivery.

## PFI projects providing or involving real estate

### Central and local government accommodation

Central government projects include large high-profile examples such as GCHQ where the GSL consortium of Tarmac, Group 4 and BT are in detailed negotiations. This project is based on the provision of new accommodation and services at the GCHQ site in Benhall, Cheltenham. Local government projects include the North Wiltshire District Council accommodation project to rationalise and replace old space on a number of sites in Chippenham.

### Education

The Colfox School scheme in Dorset is one of the projects most referred to. It is also one of the earliest. Loughton School in Essex and Leyton School in Waltham Forest are projects seeing bidder shortlisting during 1999.

### Health

The Department of Health has focused attention on a reduced number of larger PFI schemes. These include the new Edinburgh

Royal Infirmary and the Hereford Hospitals NHS Trust. In the latter example Mercia Healthcare Ltd has signed a 30-year contract to provide and refurbish hospital services. A new 250-bed acute unit will form the centre of the 340-bed hospital. Mercia Healthcare is a project company formed by a grouping of Alfred McAlpine, W.S. Atkins, Gardner Merchant and Norweb. The Hereford scheme is also a good example of PFI on a brownfield site. Many PFI schemes have been constructed on greenfield sites because of risk transfer issues and the tight project timespan which can make the clean-up of contaminated sites unfeasible. The site used in the Hereford project has had a variety of uses including that of a slaughterhouse.

A further health sector example is the New Royal Infirmary of Edinburgh. The project provides a new 869-bed teaching hospital, a medical school, 24 operating theatres and a patient hotel. Clinical services include centralised imaging, liver and renal transplant, cardiology, neonatology and obstetrics. The capital cost exceeds £200 million and the project utilises a 70-acre (25.82-hectare) greenfield site.

The largest PFI health sector project to date is the 1,000-bed hospital for the South Tees Acute Hospitals NHS Trust.

The Department of Health also procures a large number of non-real estate based projects via the PFI. A number of NHS trusts are procuring Pathology Information Management Systems, for example.

## Lord Chancellor's Department

The Lord Chancellor's Department is sourcing magistrates' court projects through the PFI. Examples include those in Merseyside, East Anglia and Derbyshire.

## Social housing

North East Derbyshire District Council is one example of a body which has used the PFI to provide social housing. In the subject case a small transaction having a value in the region of £2 million was concluded with South Yorkshire Housing Association.

## MoD

Projects under the direction of the MoD include the £300 million GCHQ project mentioned earlier. Smaller projects include the married quarters at Yeovilton involving Western Challenge Housing Association.

## DETR including highways and infrastructure projects

A range of projects have been procured through PFI, including various London Underground projects, the British Transport Police Central London HQ, and the Bournemouth Borough Council Library project.

## Home Office

These range across Home Office functions to include the Greater Manchester Fire Service Divisional HQ, the Norfolk Constabulary HQ and Operations Centre, and Agecroft Prison, Salford. One project of particular note is the Cumbria Police project at Workington, which involves the use of the public sector in the service provision (cleaning, etc), as it is one of the first projects where this has occurred.

## Other projects

The range includes the Foreign and Commonwealth Berlin Embassy project, the Brent street lighting scheme and the Maidstone Borough Council car parks scheme. Portsmouth City Council have provided schools, Westminster City Council residential homes, and elsewhere a number of leisure and heritage-based projects are also being discussed.

The range of projects requiring real estate input is potentially large. However, the input is often not of the magnitude which many in the property and construction professions would wish to see. The property and construction sectors must play their part. It is important also for the public sector client to understand the true worth of a lateral-thinking property professional in the project team. Many transactions have been kept on track because of the deal-making approach of the sector and a greater understanding of construction, secured lending and property assets in general.

The RICS has produced introductory guidance on the PFI, which is the starting point for those wishing to understand the involvement those in the property and construction sectors may have in the PFI process.[3] In considering the appointment of professional advisers the public sector client should also consider the guidance issued by the Treasury Taskforce.[4] In this guidance experience of the PFI process and a competency to deal with the issues the project under consideration may raise are stressed.

## Chapter 3

# The PFI process in detail: from *OJEC* notice to signing the contract

## *OJEC* notices

The majority of the work undertaken in getting a project to the stage of being *OJEC* advertised will have been undertaken by the public sector. Prior to the Bates Report many projects were advertised in *OJEC* which stood little realistic chance of being completed. Private sector players entered the field and spent time and money working up proposals only for the project to stall. The Bates Review recommended certainty and this has been introduced to a large extent with those projects that are now *OJEC* advertised. These projects have been approved and there is more certainty that bidders are bidding for projects which will actually happen.

The government has increasingly wished to see a standardisation of advertisements within *OJEC*. The wording of the advertisement will depend on the procurement procedure chosen. For works, services and supply contracts, European Community procurement policy specifies three types of procedure: the open procedure, the restricted procedure and the negotiated procedure. Almost all PFI contracts will be procured using the negotiated procedure. A large element of competition will be introduced into the process in order to give value for money.

If a prior information notice (PIN) is published in *OJEC* the Treasury Taskforce has issued standard wording for the notice. This reads, 'Potential suppliers who wish to register an interest in this requirement may now do so and will, in return, receive an Information Memorandum outlining the nature of the project and its scope. Suppliers should note that this requirement is considered suitable for the application of the Private Finance Initiative (PFI) or an alternative Public Private Partnership (PPP).' Prior Information Notices, in common with *OJEC* notices, are made available on a number of websites. Some sites charge for access, however; the Treasury Taskforce site at http://www.treasury-projects-taskforce.gov.uk makes the information freely available.

In deciding to respond to an *OJEC* notice the work of the bidder begins in earnest. The advice has already been offered that bidders ought to decide which type, size, nature and location of project is for them. Selecting projects, which meet predetermined business strategies, is advisable. Later sections explore some of the issues surrounding project type, size and location. The focus of this chapter is to assume that the project is worthwhile and that you would like to be successful in your bid.

The Bates Review brought in a level of standardisation to the description of PFI projects within an *OJEC* notice. The *OJEC* notice will state a publication date and various other standardised references relating to the author of the notice, the reference and the project type. A text will follow which is the meat of the notice. This will state the awarding authority, which is important for issues of client covenant and project sector selection. The means of awarding the contract will be stated. This may or may not be accelerated in procedure depending upon the nature of the project. (Many education sector projects are accelerated, and PFI has yet to find an alternative to the September completion deadline prevalent for projects in the sector.) The type of contract on offer will make clear reference to the PFI principles and process. The site of the works or a location for the service provision will be stated. Government policy on this issue has altered over time. Originally site-specific *OJEC* notices were deemed to go against the policy of securing best value. Subsequently many bodies have wished to specify the site upon which the service should take place. This is again common in the education sector. It is likely that we will see a split between site-specific *OJEC* notices for projects such as schools and wider *OJEC* notices for accommodation projects.

The works required together with an estimated value will be stated in the *OJEC* notice. Comment will be made as to whether the project can be divided into lots (unlikely for a PFI project). The deadline and address for receipt of applications will be given. Information may be given on the legal form which a bidder is required to take and reference may be made to the need for deposits or guarantees. Qualifications are likely to be sought; these will be obtained from a detailed questionnaire sent out to respondents, completion of which is discussed in more detail in the next chapter. A reference may be made to the acceptability or otherwise of variants. Usually variants will be acceptable in order to encourage private sector innovation. The Treasury Taskforce has again recommended standard wording to cover variant bids, namely 'Variant bids will be permissible, provided the contracting authority agrees that the core requirements will be met.' (The wording is provided on the Internet at http://www.treasury-projects-taskforce.gov.uk/series_3/technote2/2tech_08.htm.)

The above together with the language required to be used in the response (English) will be the core content of a project *OJEC* notice. The amount of technical information may vary yet the notice will outline the core elements of the project. If these core elements change too widely the public sector client may be forced to recommence the process and advertise the contract again. The right content in the *OJEC* notice is therefore very important to the public sector.

The regulations relating to *OJEC* notices are available from the Stationery Office. The basic format can, however, be obtained from looking at other recent *OJEC* advertisements. The Treasury Task-force website at http://www.treasury-projects-taskforce.gov.uk is again recommended.

What is required in response to an *OJEC* notice may vary. The *OJEC* notice is seeking expressions of interest. A simple initial letter or telephone call will lead to the dispatch of information about the project. However, it is strongly recommended that the expression of interest be made in writing in addition to any discussion which may take place. A discussion with the client project manager at this stage can prove very useful. Certain strengths and weaknesses of the project may be identified, and positively taking an interest at this stage can enhance the initial bid response.

Care should be taken on the side of the bidder to ensure that the best placed individual makes the initial contact. An understanding of the PFI is very important. A construction company marketing person may find him or herself talking to a client side project manager who has an accountancy background, so the concerns of the two will be different. However, the client is always right, and an understanding of the problems of the client will be more effective than engaging in construction speak about projects being on time and within budget.

## The briefing day

The public sector client may hold a briefing day at which the client's project team will introduce the proposed site or project. An attendance list will almost certainly be kept and one question on the bid response form may well relate to attendance at the briefing day. One aim of the briefing day concept was to enable networking between interested parties in a project to assist in the formation of consortia. However, in the author's experience the seeds of most consortia are sowed prior to the briefing day through existing working arrangements, or after the briefing day if it becomes apparent that the project team needs strengthening in order to improve the chances of becoming preferred bidder. It is beneficial to attend a briefing day, but those who have not yet done so should prepare themselves for the psychology inherent in this type of event. A range of parties are likely to be present – local contractors, national contractors, professional advisers, bankers and perhaps some direct property interests. Service providers may be present depending upon the type and size of the project. It is worth sounding out who is there for what reason. A banker may be there because they have experience in the sector. They may play a direct role in a consortium yet may be more likely to be advertising a willingness in principle to be involved in projects of this type. Merchant banks are more likely to be present, and though they will prove expensive sources of finance for smaller projects, they are worth talking to at events such as this.

Contractors at a briefing day will fall into one of two groups: those hoping to lead a consortium to build the construction output, and those who decide that they cannot form a consortium but who hope to pick up the construction as part of a later tendering process. Whether the construction output is subsequently tendered will depend on which party becomes the preferred bidder and which party actually completes the deal.

Professional advisers at a briefing day are likely to be piecing a bid together or to be representing an interest on a basis that has already been agreed. There is considerable merit in an interested party with little experience of the PFI employing professionals who have experience. Standard questions on the response form will relate to experience of the type of project in question and to experience of the PFI as a method of service provision. The ability to answer (honestly) as many questions as possible in a positive fashion will assist with the bid.

## The selection process

### Compliance

The selection process to reduce the number of interested parties is likely to start with an assessment of compliance. Has all the requested information been supplied? Was the expression made in the appropriate format in the agreed time? Was the expression sent to the right party? The expression of interest should be checked for compliance. A non-compliant bid is the easiest for a public sector body to take no further.

## Analysing bidder questionnaires

After the non-compliant bids have been removed from the process the next stage will be to score the answers to the response questionnaire. European law kicks in quite heavily at this point. Subjectivity should be removed from the process as far as possible. So a scoring system is likely to be used by the public sector body. While these have varied from project to project, they generally award favourable answers with a point. A particularly strong response may gain an additional point while a particularly weak answer may see a point lost. The extent to which points can be lost or additional points awarded will depend on the legal advice received by the client at that time. The main point to remember is that the process should be open to scrutiny and this will imply the need for a quantitative technique. Qualitative issues are more likely to be addressed initially by the question of bid compliance. A small number of 'points' can stand between elimination and progression to the next stage. Care should be taken to pick up all those points that it is possible for the bidder to collect.

The relatively small difference between a bid that survives the cut and one which does not has led to the use of scenario questions. These have to operate within the required legal framework and be open to scrutiny. Too great a reliance on the answers would give a public sector client a legal headache if challenged. The use of these questions, while qualitative, should still be approached in a quantitative manner.

The procedure at this stage may be in the form of an invitation to submit outline proposals (ISOP stage).

## Invitation to submit outline proposals

At this point there will be a breakdown of the evaluation criteria against assessment areas. It is important to consider the likely evaluation criteria and the assessment areas. The former may include the following:

- innovation;
- compatibility with operational approach;
- deliverability;
- flexibility;
- risk transfer.

The assessment areas will vary to some degree depending upon the nature of the project. They may include the following:

- risk transfer;
- planning/site considerations;
- design (diagrams/sketches);
- decant;
- redundant premises;
- consequential risk;
- occupancy risk;
- development risk;
- programme;
- accommodation requirements;
- facilities management;
- alternative revenue streams;
- contract framework;
- consortium structure.

The above are actual criteria and assessment areas which have been used in projects and highlight the importance of risk transfer to the process. For each of the assessment areas a matrix box can be constructed against the evaluation criteria using the questions and points sought within each assessment area. For example, within the contract framework assessment area five points may arise against which the outline proposal is assessed, as follows:

1 Demonstration of an understanding of the contractual issues.
2 Position on liquidated damages.
3 Position on performance-related deductions against the unitary charge.
4 Acceptance of change of law risk.
5 Position on collateral warranties.

The above points may appear on one side of a matrix box with the evaluation criteria on the other side. Those criteria which are inappropriate to the assessment question would be removed or blanked out. For example, the position on liquidated damages is unlikely to be assessed against 'innovation'. Criteria such as innovation will be much more important in areas like alternative revenue stream assessment and occupancy risk assessment.

Having created a full matrix to deal with all the assessment areas and assessment criteria the client's project team will need to score the evaluation. This may be carried out in a number of ways. However, it is likely that a positive scoring system will be used with 0 being awarded for a point which is unaddressed, 1 being awarded for an unsatisfactory answer, 2 for a satisfactory answer, 3 for a good answer and 4 for an excellent answer. On this basis of evaluation the bulk of the scoring can be expected to be 0, 1 or 2. A few answers may receive a 3 and very few a 4. With known assessment areas and criteria the art is to move all your answers up the scoring grid. It is highly recommended that you use the experience of your team to leave no likely point unaddressed and attempt to provide satisfactory answers wherever possible. However, remember that your stance on a point at the ISOP stage may be expected to remain in later phases of the process. A dim view would be taken of a party who agrees to absorb all risk at the ISOP stage and then moves back substantially from this at the ITN or preferred bidder stage.

When each assessment area and all criteria have been assessed the results will be totalled in order to provide a decision-making tool for moving to the next stage of the process. An overview may, however, be taken to ensure that a bidder does not score too poorly against any one evaluation criteria or in any one assessment area.

Different members of the client's project team will wish to see positive responses in different areas. While something of a holistic view must be taken. It would be difficult to score well in all areas except FM in which all answers were unsatisfactory and expect to be selected for the next stage of the process. This may happen but the weakness would have to be quickly and decisively addressed.

The PFI process attempts to be fair yet no system is perfect. One of the main difficulties for those with little experience of PFI is to gain that experience in the first instance. The PFI response process for many projects would also appear to favour the grouping of parties within a bid at an earlier point. The combined experience of constituent players can be drawn on rather than the experience of one organisation alone. It is often the case that combined organisations have more experience than any one player within the group.

If you have little experience of PFI it is suggested that you link with those that have. The other approach for companies with a proven track record in a field and little experience of PFI is to be open about the lack of experience. State that advisers with experience will be brought in and stress that value for money will be offered due to the fact that the bid will be made competitive. An apparent financial loss leader for gains elsewhere is hard to ignore if the company proposing the solution provides a very good covenant.

## After the initial response and long list selection

The ethos of the PFI process is to move to a short list and the issuing of an invitation to tender (ITT) as soon as is practically possible. How this is achieved will depend on the number and quality of the bid responses. It will also depend on the criteria which the public sector client has laid down. If you pass the first cut and the ISOP stage the next stage is likely to be the invitation to tender (ITT). The replies to the ITT will be assessed and judged against criteria. A number of bidders will then be selected to move forward to the invitation to negotiate (ITN) stage. The number at this stage will usually be in the order of three. This was the case, for example, in the Norfolk Constabulary Headquarters Project. From the responses to the ITN a preferred bidder and possibly a reserve preferred bidder would be selected. Most advisers with experience of the PFI process would advise the public sector client to select a formal reserve and to notify the parties of the guidelines during which the roles of the preferred and reserve bidders may change. From the public sector viewpoint competition should remain for as long as possible. The private sector preference is to reach preferred bidder status as quickly as possible with no reserve in place. If no reserve is in place it can be difficult for the public sector client to change bidders as the whole process may have to be started afresh. The public sector client is likely to find the project timetable slip rapidly without an effective reserve bidder who can also theoretically become the preferred bidder.

To be an unsuccessful reserve bidder is the worst of positions for the private sector. Any party that reaches this stage will have invested a considerable amount of time and resources. Various suggestions have been put forward for the aggregation of costs to provide some form of compensation to the unsuccessful party. However, as the public sector often asks for a contribution to their development costs which is not usually supported, there is little realistic scope for bidder costs to be refunded in whole or in part at present. With certain large public/private schemes some provision may be made for a proportion of bidder costs to be met. Six bidders involved with the London Underground project have spent over £10 million between them. Some of this will be rebated, yet a large element of the cost of bidding will remain with the bidders. The public sector client costs are even greater, the initial role and cost of Price Waterhouse Coopers mushrooming greatly (see *Hansard*, Parliamentary questions tabled by John Redwood MP).

Jumping the hurdles of the ITT and the ITN are extensions of the initial selection process. They are, however, more involved and will be project-specific. Although we can consider a number of general points to increase selection prospects, there is, however, a lot to be gained from utilising the knowledge of an adviser who has experience of that project type. Experience on the public sector client side is particularly valuable as it will provide an insight to the thinking of the decision-making body.

## The invitation to tender

An invitation to tender will be issued to a specified number of parties. At this stage draft project documentation will be issued and the bidders will be asked to comment on the acceptability or otherwise of certain contract clauses. This point in the process is also the start point for each of the bidders to give some serious thought to the financial position. Until this point the amount of the single unitary charge and other financial questions will not have been the main driving force in the selection process. At this point financial issues are weighted much more strongly in the selection process.

## The invitation to negotiate

This is the period of time given to the parties left at this stage to refine their bids in the light of more detailed project information. The client may well have organised a number of project days to focus on particular aspects of the project. Technical issues, legal issues and redundant property issues all formed the basis for information briefings to assist the bidders to arrive at a best bid in the Norfolk Constabulary HQ project. The invitation to negotiate stage also enables the financial advisers to ensure that affordability thresholds are likely to be met in the best and final offers.

## Best and final offers

This is the period of time for each of the bidders to prepare and submit their best and final offer. The financial criteria in the decision-making process will have reached a high at this point.

## Preferred bidder selection

This is the choice based on the best and final offer (or tender revision) of one party with whom the contract will be negotiated through to financial close. As suggested elsewhere, from the public sector viewpoint a reserve bidder is strongly recommended.

## Financial close

Unfortunately all projects have taken some time to reach financial close. This can be frustrating for both parties to the contract. The lawyers perhaps have a vested interest in spending large amounts of time worrying about minor points which are unlikely to be material in the context of the contract but while some lawyers certainly have run up large fee bills others have been much more focused. A comparison of legal costs incurred by the public sector client and the preferred bidder will no doubt be undertaken. While the results of such a study may be interesting, they will only further the concentration of PFI advice in the legal field. A lawyer who knows what is material and what is not will always be preferred to one who has yet to find this out.

The public sector can be guided in the appointment of advisers by material such as the Treasury Taskforce Private Finance Technical Note 3, *How to Appoint and Manage Advisers*.[4] Asking questions at interview or on tender documentation is also a useful technique for attempting to assess competency. Ask not only whether the lawyer has dealt with a PFI contract, but also what lessons were learnt during the process. How did the final contract deal with specific issues such as the payment mechanism? Obtain from each potential adviser an indication that they appreciate and understand the issues raised by the PFI process.

The private sector should seek advice from a similarly experienced lawyer. A commercial awareness and attitude is perhaps an attribute that should be tested. The result should be that the lawyer responds appropriately to each stage of the selection process. The work required will be greatest during the later stages of the selection process.

If both parties have advisers who have reached financial close in respect of another project this will be of considerable mutual comfort.

## The timescale

The time it takes for a project to proceed through the above stages will depend on many factors including the complexity of the project and the willingness of both parties to make it happen. The New Royal Infirmary of Edinburgh project gives an idea of how drawn out the process can be for a large project:

| | |
|---|---|
| PFI feasibility study | September 1994 |
| Appointment of advisers | September 1994 to June 1995 |
| Preparation of medical brief | January to December 1995 |
| Short list consortia | May 1995 |
| Prepare tender documentation | July 1995 to January 1996 |
| Issue tender documents | January 1996 |
| Return of tenders | June 1996 |
| Receipt of revised bids | August 1996 |
| Selection of preferred bidder | October 1996 |
| Full business case completed | December 1996 |
| Approvals | April to September 1997 |
| Financial close | August 1998 |

Other projects have learned the lessons of earlier projects to shorten the time spent on various activities. For example, in the Norfolk Constabulary HQ project a much shorter time period was allocated for the preparation of tender documents and their initial consideration. However, in this project, like many others, the programme slipped in the later stages. Projects now coming through the system are moving at a greater pace. There is often an incentive for the public sector to make sure their project is ahead of others competing for the same department funding allocation, although the Treasury still encounters problems with programme slippage and the timespan between consent for the *OJEC* notice, the issue of a promissory note and the actual drawdown of funds.

## Chapter 4

# Bidder evaluation in more detail

## Introduction

A work of this size cannot hope to cover all aspects of bidder evaluation or the converse, jumping the hurdles to financial close. However, looking in further detail at areas of importance in the selection process will help to reinforce some of the concepts of the PFI. This chapter looks at a number of issues which bidders will have to address at some point in the selection process. It is hoped that this chapter will offer some practical focus for those actually working on a project. For those reading this work on the public sector side the points identified in this chapter are some of those which it is likely will need to be addressed. Each project is different and each client will have particular ideas about how they would like to see their development take shape. There are, however, a large number of common concerns to all PFI projects and a range of concerns specific to projects of a particular type.

As noted, the particular project is clearly important. Is there a theme to the project? Are there service issues to be addressed? Can the ethos of the project support the aim and mission statement of the body in question? Attempt to draw from the culture of the organisation and incorporate the positive attributes in the proposals for the project. If the organisation is seeking a radical change and wishes to move away from that with which it is associated again this spirit can be reflected in the ethos of the scheme.

It is likely that a number of similar projects will have been undertaken either by means of the PFI or a Public Private Partnership, or on a traditional basis. Find out from the public sector which of these similar schemes they admire and which they dislike. It would be helpful to gauge these points from an operational level as well as a decision-making level. In some projects the operational considerations have such an importance that the role of elected members tends to follow the operational advice given. With other project types the elected members may have their own strong views. These views may need to be assuaged or alternatively projects in sectors in which political interference is common may need to be approached differently or not at all.

## Planning and site considerations

The *OJEC* notice may specify site considerations, for example that the site chosen for the project is within six miles of a particular mainline railway station. The extent to which the *OJEC* notice will stipulate a specific area or even a specific site will depend on the project type. In any event compliance will be required with the locational and site considerations specified in the *OJEC* notice.

The site will need to be deliverable. This deliverability can be viewed in a number of ways. The site should be capable of housing the project in terms of site size and also in the ability to obtain planning permission. An existing development site identified in the Local Plan for a particular area will be more deliverable than an opportunistic site awaiting hopeful inclusion in a Local Plan review some three years hence. By all means include this option as a variant but do not rely upon it in the first instance.

There may be access or other restrictions which need to be addressed. For example, projects in the police sector will need to have regard to the *Police Buildings Design Guide*[5] which stipulates a number of requirements for police buildings of certain types, eg a primary and secondary point of access is required. A school project may need to be situated in a locality to serve a given catchment area. This is so likely that with many school projects the education authority will have identified a particular site. Again, while variants may be put forward, a core scheme will be required on the chosen site.

## Design

The amount of detail necessary in connection with the design of the proposed project will increase at each stage of the selection process. At the first expression of interest stage it may only be necessary to show that a party capable of building design is a member of the team. At the ISOP stage the public sector client is likely to require site layout information. Have any locality constraints placed in the original *OJEC* notice been observed? Is it clear that the proposal will 'work' on the chosen site? Is the site large enough? Does it have the necessary access? Is the nature of the proposal such that it is likely to receive planning permission? Some diagrammatic sketches are also recommended, even if these were not expressly called for, to show functional and aspirational requirements. These may need to be refined but can be used to show an understanding of the client's operational needs or a desire to learn to appreciate the same.

The understanding of operational need in a design context will need to be much greater as ITT and ITN stages are reached. The designer should be capable of listening to and absorbing what is required. One outcome of the PFI process is a definite drive towards designing buildings in a practical fashion. They should not necessarily be built to the lowest common denominator in terms of design quality, but they should be fit for the purpose for which they are designed (and fit also for a range of alternative uses in an ideal world).

## Decant

There will need to be an understanding of the client requirements by the potential bidders. Which functions are required to be kept operational? Which functions can be allowed some down-time? For those functions that can be allowed some down-time, what is the maximum period that can be given? There will be a range of issues to be understood by the bidders, and these will need to be reflected in the approach to decant the move from the existing accommodation to the new. Competent proposals and timescales are a must, supported ideally by project flow charts and details of comparable examples.

## Redundant premises

The particular project may give rise to a number of redundant or surplus properties and it may be necessary to bring forward proposals for dealing with these buildings. Certain of the properties may be freehold or long leasehold and would stand as assets which could be expected to realise a value, while other property may be short leasehold in nature. There may be outstanding dilapidation or other problems and these properties may constitute a liability.

The exact nature, title and terms of any property held should be considered. Is it an asset for which proposals can be developed to maximise its value, or is it a liability? In respect of all property consider when it may be best disposed off, not just having regard to market conditions but also by looking at its use in the decant process. The method of disposal is worthy of further thought:

realise any development potential, yet work with the public sector client in apportioning the uplift benefit.

The best application of funds from redundant property disposals is likely to be in reducing the single unitary charge and in making the project more affordable. Consider therefore how the assets and liabilities may be timed to fit in with the funding, decant and charging for the space, to best effect.

## Programme

The public sector client is likely to issue a programme, or at least a target date, for when they would like the facility to be fully operational. Initial scoring is likely to favour positive responses to meeting the programme as set out. If, however, the programme is unlikely to be capable of being met, do find a way of discussing this with the client's project advisers. School projects are always needed for a September deadline. It may be crucial to do all you can to agree to meet the project deadline, yet if it becomes apparent that this just cannot be met both sides to the project should work together to find the best solution. An element of realism with regard to the timescale will also be required on the public sector side.

## Accommodation requirements

These, like the proposals for the design of the building, will need to evolve as one moves through the bidding process. Consider first all the guidance offered by the public sector body: to what extent has it told you what it wants and how it wants the accommodation to be arranged? Is there any guidance to which you ought to refer, the *Police Buildings Design Guide*[5] or a particular local authority's standards for school building, for example?

It will be necessary to demonstrate a relationship between the various areas of the accommodation in a manner that assists the working relationship of the departments and functions within. Find out which departments or functions are required to be proximate to each other and which are best located further away. Reflect in the process the likely requirement to increase or decrease the amount of space occupied. This may be the amount of space occupied in total or the amount of space of different general types. The churn flexibility (the ability of the structure and its layout to accommodate space planning and other changes) will help the user; it should also help in the overall project proposal.

Ensure as the process evolves that the necessary services provision will be made available to the different areas of accommodation. Different standards may be set for various items such as the lux level of room lighting: consider the minimum requirement and also the potential need for future change.

## Facilities management/operation of the contract

The operational phase of the contract carries a considerable percentage of the total project cost. While it is unlikely that the facilities management phase will carry quite the same weighting in the selection process, the importance of the issues will be reflected in the choice of the preferred bidder. If the FM provider is weak this may affect the bankability of the whole project. Consider also the cost structure and inherent efficiencies or inefficiencies of the particular FM provider.

It will be necessary to understand the nature of the services which are to be provided and to be able to demonstrate an acceptable method of delivering them to the required standard. Exceeding minimum standards may offer some comfort that in the event of minor default the minimum standard may still be exceeded.

The FM process will need to be managed and controlled, and there will need to be a method by which faults are reported, the situation noted and the fault rectified. A number of interrelated issues are brought out here: the charging process, the penalty deduction process, contract monitoring to record the actual position and quality control to reduce the likelihood of poor performance.

As the selection process moves on it will be necessary to identify a range of providers. A position will also need to be taken on ensuring that value for money is offered. Is there a way of market testing the service provision in the contract?

## Alternative revenue streams

A more detailed property and construction-based consideration of alternative revenue streams follows in a later chapter. One of the key aims of the PFI was to introduce the concept of alternative revenue streams and their use in bringing down the single unitary charge and in making the project more affordable. During the selection process it will therefore be necessary to show a commitment to the concept of alternative revenue streams, the means by which these will be managed and something of the range of ideas. To be of benefit to the public sector client there will need to be some form of profit-sharing arrangement. I have argued that where the revenue stream owes much of its origin to the presence of the public sector body then the income should be divided having regard to this. Similarly where the income is provided through building a separate structure which is not part of the core project, or the income stream owes little to the presence of the public sector body, then the supplier should receive a proportionately greater benefit.

## Contract framework

There is a range of contract issues within a PFI project as with any project in general. Certain contractual issues are PFI-specific, while other issues involve bringing a point, such as liquidated damages, into a PFI framework. Much of what will be requested by the public sector will derive from the lawyers attempting to protect the position in as many ways as possible. The supplier will design, build, finance and operate the building, though no doubt collateral warranties will still be sought.

Certain contract framework points will owe their origin to the thinking of the moment. The move towards standard contract templates or standard contract clauses will at least assist in identifying the drivers behind points, even if the standard clauses themselves are not adopted.

A change in the PFI process toward a greater involvement by property professionals in the process will lead to contract forms which will begin to reflect what the parties have agreed rather than an unlikely wish list. The analogy is a lease negotiation process. In a particular market, in a particular locality, at a particular time, the landlord or the tenant will have a certain negotiating strength. In a poor market the landlord can forget his desire to see a 25-year lease with five-yearly upward only rent reviews and no break clauses. The property professionals will put the deal together and advise on how the market affects the terms which can be agreed. The same should be true of the PFI process, although it is up to the property profession to show it has an important role to play in brokering the deal and the terms, and for the public sector to recognise that others besides accountants can play a part in this process.

## Consortium structure

At some point in the selection process it will be necessary for the public sector client to satisfy itself that the bidder's structure is sound. Contract linkage will need to be put in place between the various constituent partners to the bid. The public sector will need to see and understand the relationships. The consortium structure may also have a bearing on the financial power of the bidder and on the comfort that it offers to the public sector. The private sector should consider carefully the tax treatment of the vehicle used to supply the product and service.

## Acceptance and transfer of various forms of risk

Issues relating to risk and risk transfer are covered from a property and construction viewpoint in Chapter 7.

## Affordability

The project will have to be affordable for the public sector client to progress further. Enhancing affordability and what makes a project more affordable are considered in Chapter 5.

## Value for money

In addition to being affordable the project will also need to offer value for money or best value.

## Chapter 5

# Alternative revenue streams and enhancing affordability

Third-party revenue streams, or alternative revenue streams, have been the poor performers in many PFI/PPP schemes. The idea is sound yet the application has been weak. We may expect to see more effort being made to enhance third-party revenue streams in existing projects as a way of increasing profitability. In projects that are presently being brought forward bidder's may need to place more effort in considering alternative revenue stream options.

## The nature of alternative revenue streams

Alternative revenue streams may flow from the project. These can, broadly speaking, be classified into two groups. The first grouping arises from the additional use of a facility that needs to be provided as part of the project. One of the simplest would be a catering facility, the use of which is then opened up to others. The second grouping involves more lateral thought, and exists in the opportunity to create or do something which has nothing whatsoever to do with the project.

It is not the function of the legal advisers to the client to employ lateral thought in arriving at ideas for alternative revenue generation. Financial advisers in the traditional mould are often focused elsewhere, their skills tending not to be centred on opportunity realisation. When more developers become involved in real estate PFI/PPP schemes the situation may improve. A public sector client may find the bidding team more imaginative if a developer or development surveyor is part of it. Developers are, however, a special breed and advisers need to understand them on their own terms.

The client described above, the public sector body, may well take the view that alternative revenue streams are for the bidder and, ultimately, the supplier to generate. This is true, yet the very viability of a number of projects at option appraisal stage may

Every bid has a cost and a benefit, the theory being to plot these to locate the preferable bid. In the example shown below one bid does not meet the acceptable benefit threshold while one does not offer value for money. Two bids are in the area of acceptability.

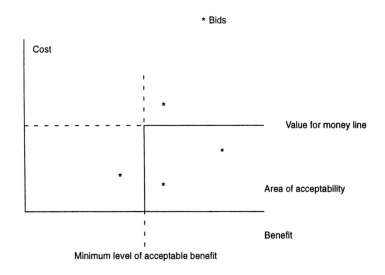

**Figure 5.1 PFI project bid plotting**

require strategic consideration of real estate assets. Alternative revenue streams may be necessary to facilitate bringing the project forward.

As noted elsewhere in this book, to be 'affordable' the public sector has to be able to pay for the project. It is generally able to do so if existing resources meet any gap in the difference between the NPV (net present value) of the standard spending assessment and the NPV of the unitary charge. Together with being affordable the project will also have to offer 'value for money' or 'best value'. In order to determine whether this exists the NPV of the unitary charge over the life of the project is compared with the NPV of the public sector comparator, discussed earlier. One can now see why what goes into forming the PSC is so important. It can make the PFI project appear better or worse in terms of value for money. Many bidders will seek to discover the terms upon which the PSC will be based, concerned that they might not be a comparison of like with like. Those worried that there may be a bias towards the PFI process have raised similar concerns. For example, Michael Ball, a governor of Pimlico School, in a letter in *The Independent*[6] commented that the public sector model contained an assumption that 50 private flats were to be constructed, while the PFI model of the preferred bidder showed 169. This is not comparing like with like. In the public sector model only 50 flats existed to be set against the cost of the school. The complaint being that the PFI model took the higher and more attractive figure of 169. The debate about the extent to which the PSC should be the same or allow for entrepreneurial improvement in circumstances will no doubt continue.

If all bids offer value for money and all are affordable, the original decision-making criteria specified in the *OJEC* notice will need to be referred to in order to decide which offers best value. It will rarely be the case that all bids at best and final offer stage will be affordable. The more affordable a bid can be made, the greater the chance of being chosen as the preferred bidder and the greater the subsequent prospects of reaching a satisfactory financial close.

Figure 5.1 illustrates graphically the concepts of cost and benefit, and the thresholds, which need to be crossed for a project to be feasible. This form of analysis can and should be applied to all of the decision-making criteria.

The cost should not merely be a financial cost. For each of the decision-making criteria a separate graph could be plotted, the final result being an aggregation.

The accounting debate (considered further in Chapter 7) and the FRS 5 situation provide another raft of reasons for alternative revenue stream income generation, to be explored more fully. A proportion of the single unitary charge must be put at risk. For those projects that have to meet the contract structure test, having a proportion of the payment at risk will be required in order to receive credit approval. There is scope in many projects to offset some or all of the income effectively put at risk by alternative revenue income. In other cases the income may be shared between the parties in an agreed manner, reducing the unitary charge and thereby making the project more affordable.

The alternative revenue stream opportunities which actually exist will depend on the project in question. The project may make surplus various fixed assets. These assets can be put in a position to yield maximum value in absolute terms. The discounting of the project cash flows should be looked at to see when disposals could best be structured given the market for the property and the effect of timing on the financial position. It is also the case that existing buildings may play a useful role in the best available decant proposition. Work may be required to establish the best planning position of surplus sites or inherent opportunities.

A review of the planned maintenance programme may also stop unnecessary spend on a building which is to change use.

## Alternative revenue identification

The first destination is the output specification: what services need to be provided in order to meet the output specification for the project? From these an assessment can be made of the likely market and user demand to establish whether any offer cost-effective opportunities for third-party income. The catering facility mentioned earlier is an obvious candidate. The location of the project will undoubtedly affect the external income-generating potential.

More unusual sources of income may come from some lateral thought. A project with a communications mast is capable of mast sharing: for a structure of sufficient height, this could yield a six-figure annual income. Use of a balancing lake could see income from fishing rights. Facilities may contain vending machines. The list of opportunities to be explored suits the creative entrepreneurial thought process of a property professional.

Having considered the proposed output specification take some time to reflect on the anticipated design solution. Surveyors have long worked with architects and developers to ensure that space is best designed to fit the likely prevailing property market. A PFI/PPP scheme should be no different. The contract will probably provide for variations in the amount of space occupied. If any becomes surplus that should be capable of some beneficial use. The nature of these uses and the potential for others will vary widely based on the nature of the local property market. This point has been little explored by the accountancy profession in their treatment of risk to date. We consider some of the issues raised in the sections dealing with risk contained in this book.

All areas of the form and function of the building can be explored for income prospects, as can the uses to which the facility will be put. If the facility is to be commercially intensive in any area (eg photographic production or reprographics), it may be that this function can be restructured or expanded.

The PFI project team should include individuals capable of lateral thought if a bid is to be constructed which is the most affordable and offers the best value.

## Chapter 6

# Facilities management: the operational phase of the contract

## Introduction

The operational phase is the most important part of any PFI contract. It is the phase during which the bidder delivers and the client receives the service specified in the output specification. In Chapter 1 it was noted that some 70 per cent of project cost might be attributed to this phase, and by far the majority of the payment under the contract will be to offset these costs and to provide for a profit on this activity. The financing banks to a successful consortium pay particular regard to the facilities management provision. More than one preferred bidder has lost that status or been unable to complete due to the unbankability of the FM provider in place.

Choosing the right FM provider is critical to the success of a PFI project. Almost all PFI projects will involve a mixture of debt and equity finance. Much of the debt finance is likely to come from a bank lending in this field (or in respect of larger projects via a merchant bank syndicating the loan among other banks). The bank will wish to see security of income. Under the terms of a PFI contract a proportion of the single unitary charge payment must be put at risk. If the services are not provided in the stipulated fashion then the payments under the contract will reduce. Banks therefore pay particular attention to the element of the payment that is put at risk and to how likely the supplier is not to receive the same.

The contract will provide for termination and step-in rights in the most extreme of circumstances. When service breaches reach a specified level and remain for a given period of time the public sector body will wish to remedy matters themselves. Funding banks would wish to prevent this happening, as the income stream, which is behind the loan, will be affected.

The service contract will be in place for some 25 or 30 years. The creditworthiness of the FM supplier is therefore far more important than may be initially apparent. The FM supplier and the income under this part of the contract are the single most important factors in gauging whether bank debt finance will be secured.

FM providers may be grouped according to their size, background and how they perform the service. The first grouping includes sizeable publicly quoted companies, for example Rentokil, who own a number of subsidiary companies which between them can provide most, if not all, of the specified services. The second grouping includes companies which offer a varying range of service provision and have generally been established by construction companies to broaden the base of their activities. The third grouping provides little or none of the services directly. They are those which look upon the FM provision as an extension of property management. The background is likely to be in property management or wider property services.

The above groupings are not meant to be precise nor are they meant to be absolute. It is to be expected that more players will enter the market while some will fall away. An FM provider could make a bid for a contractor; similarly certain contractors may pursue FM business more vigorously – Amey, for example, have a stated aim in this direction. The purpose of categorising FM providers in this way is to provide an introduction to their approach and cost structure. An FM provider having a property management background may be able to compete effectively on projects which involve a number of smaller buildings or which are situated close to their office. The economic structure of this type of FM provision does not suit all projects. There is no point in paying party X an hourly rate fee for them to source the work from party Y when a third party is able to manage and perform the task directly at a lower cost and at no lesser quality.

## The services to be provided under a PFI contract

These will of course vary from contract to contract. However, the differences are becoming more sectoral rather than between projects of the same type. A certain level of risk transfer will need to be achieved and this will occur (in part) by the provision of a certain basket of services. Within the field of service provision another glossary of terms has been developed which will need to be understood by those performing the contract as well as those negotiating it.

The first distinction is to define where the service provision by the FM provider starts and stops. For example, with a hospital project the FM provision will not extend to clinical services. With an educational project it is highly unlikely to include the provision of teaching staff. However, with a prison or secure accommodation project the service provision may well include the operational supervision of people housed in the facility.

The output specification for service provision issued by the public sector body will create the starting point. However, that body will have to transfer sufficient services to ensure adequate risk transfer has taken place. The extent of service provision provided for in other projects within the same sector will provide a good understanding of the likely base of service provision. An FM provider can always seek guidance from the relevant government department as to the scope of service provision in signed projects. This may create an initial understanding as to whether the subject project is seeking too much or too little in terms of service provision. Bear in mind also that if for good economic reasons or for reasons of alternative revenue income, the bidder can supply additional services to offer best value, then this should be suggested. There may be good reasons why the public sector body does not wish to extend the scope of service provision. However, if so doing can make the project more affordable the reasons for the initial decision may alter.

The concept of hard and soft services may arise from an early stage in bidder selection. All services will need to be priced and arrangements will need to be made for the periodic replacement of items. Furthermore, the service which is to be provided under the PFI contract may already be being provided in another location. Soft services, for example furniture, will be dealt with differently to the fabric of the building, which is a hard service. Again the public sector output specification will provide the first indicator of the required hard and soft services. The FM provider can, however, expect to have to work up a detailed document setting out the scope of FM provision and the pricing structure. This is likely to arise at the best and final offers (BAFO) stage and will be necessary to ensure compliance with the output specification and to provide detail on pricing structure and fault remedy procedures and timescales.

If the FM provider is part of a consortium the other members may wish to work up the scope of FM provision jointly, or to at least take advice as to the likely content. The scope of the FM provision will also be of concern to funders as noted earlier. The art is to get the balance between providing that which the public sector body wants and that which the public sector body requires for reasons of risk transfer (because the two may not be the same) while still providing value for money and affordability. If service provision can lead to alternative sources of income this may help increase affordability if some of this income is given over to the public sector body to reduce the single unitary charge. Unfortunately, banks will differ in their approach to alternative revenue income and the security with which they regard the same. Alternative revenue income is an important part of the PFI process and provides an area for property people to excel – this is discussed separately in other chapters of this book.

## The services: how they are priced, judged and the principles of their contractual treatment

The services will be those defined in the output specification which is carried throughout the contract negotiation process and incorporated in the final signed agreement. There must be risk transfer in terms of service provision and part of the bidder selection process will include determining just how much risk transfer is on offer.

A typical PFI contract will specify a range of services and the extent to which they are critical. Remedy periods will be negotiated for each of the particular service functions. A critical room may need to be returned to full working order within three hours; a non-critical room may have a problem rectification period of 12 hours. After these time periods have elapsed if the problem has not been rectified a penalty will be introduced. Whether this penalty is actual or notional will depend on how the contract is drawn. In certain contracts any failure to remedy within the stated period will lead to a deduction in the single unitary charge which is to be paid. In other contracts services will be grouped into types or areas and a deduction may only apply to an agreed figure deemed to represent services within that particular area. A final approach is to log all service faults and rectification periods and to make a deduction from the unitary charge when the service standard falls below an agreed percentage, often 95 per cent.

What is agreed may reflect all of the above approaches. A critical service may well lead to a direct deduction if there is a failure to deliver or to rectify within the agreed time period. Non-critical services are likely to have a cut-off point before a deduction is made. However, a time factor is likely to be introduced. If the poor service or service fault occurs again within a given period (that quarter for example), then a deduction will be made.

Some grouping of services is inevitable and this can lead to different treatment within different areas. PFI exists to provide the physical building and the specified services within. There is likely to be a different treatment of building faults to faults of soft service provision.

## Payment mechanism

The payment mechanism within the contract will provide for a number of payment areas. These are discussed in outline below.

### Availability payment

Accommodation is to be provided which will need to be made 'available'. When accommodation is available a payment will be made relating to the availability. It is normal for a schedule of accommodation to be agreed which defines standards to be achieved in order for that accommodation to be deemed to be 'available'. The standards will relate to matters such as heating, lighting, equipment provision, etc. The schedule and the standards will be agreed during the process leading to contractual close.

### Performance payment

If the contract structure test is required to be met by the particular project it will be necessary to put an element of the payment at risk for failures in performance. It will be necessary for all projects to achieve risk transfer, therefore it is necessary in all cases to link a proportion of the payment to performance. A proportion of the payment will therefore be a performance payment. The private sector has tried to make performance payments apply in both directions, ie increases as well as decreases. From the public sector viewpoint this has been resisted. What can, however, be negotiated is the use of performance increases above that expected which do add value to be placed in credit against certain possible payment deductions elsewhere.

### Transaction/volume payment

Volume risk is one of the risks that will be apportioned in the PFI process. The public sector client will have some idea of the volume of the service it requires in year one (how many prison places or classroom places for example). However, the number of prisoners or students may change; there is therefore a volume risk. Prisoner numbers may increase or decrease. The contract will need to provide for some flexibility. The more the private sector can absorb the volume risk the more they will be accepting a transfer of risk from the public sector. Linked with the volume of the service provided may be a volume payment: if the public sector client is not consuming so much of a particular resource it will prefer not to pay for it. In the Colfox School scheme volume risk remained with Dorset County Council. However, in an increasing number of schemes currently being worked upon a degree of volume risk is being placed on the private sector. The private sector can manage these risks by careful project selection and even turn risk into opportunity – see Chapter 7 on risk and property in PFI.

## Timing of payment

In any contract there will need to be an agreement as to the timing of payments. The timing of payments can affect quite dramatically the affordability model. From the private sector viewpoint regard will need to be given to how the project is being financed. The timing of payments can make a difference to the project viability. There may also be within the contract provision for different timings of payment dependent upon certain services being provided or not. One way in which the public sector can increase the performance pressure on the private sector is to stipulate fixed-point payment dates for all correctly functioning services in that period, services not provided to standard or requiring deduction becoming payable at a later date.

## Payment due to modifications

Either during the course of construction or within the operational phase of the contract the public sector body may require changes to be made. The contract documentation structure should provide for these and also provide a mechanism by which they are charged. The provisions may be expanded to cover the circumstance in which the private sector does not wish to undertake the change but the public sector is at liberty to undertake the same itself.

## Chapter 7

# Risk and property in PFI

There has been some considerable debate to date about the nature of risk and what risk actually is. The PFI process talks of the need for risk transfer, either to meet the contract structure test (or another stipulated requirement) or to offer value for money. Risk is also talked about in the context of FRS 5 (Financial Reporting Statement 5) and whether a project is on or off balance sheet. Unfortunately the risks necessary to achieve risk transfer in one area are not the same as the risks required in another area.

## The importance of property and construction-based risks

Table 7.1 illustrates a number of areas of risk and how each risk may impact on the PFI contractor. The table is not exhaustive: it provides a basis for further consideration of property and construction-related risks.

### *The site*

Site risks have a bearing on the process of the PFI which it is difficult for those not used to development to adequately comprehend. The risks themselves will vary from project to project and may vary between those projects where a site has been identified and those where site selection is open to the bidder. With projects in which site selection can be determined by the bidder there is an obvious assessment to be made of all locations suitable for the project. The approach advocated is to start with the Local Plan for the area. An adopted Local Plan has Section 54Astatus and its content will drive the planning process. Section 54A arises due to the 1990 and 1991 Town and Country Planning Acts. Prior to this legislation there was a general presumption in favour of development. The legislation changed the presumption to one of development in accordance with an adopted Local Plan, thus giving rise to the expression Section 54A status. Almost all sites suitable for development of the given project will have an allocation for development in the Local Plan.

**Table 7.1 Areas of risk and associated impact**

| | |
|---|---|
| The site | Planning risk, title risk, contamination and site conditions |
| Construction | Time and cost overruns, inherent liabilities and defects |
| Technical | Variations to the forecast performance of plant and changes in plant life |
| Revenue risk | Volume and use shortfalls |
| Residual value risk | That the value of the asset on reversion is lower than expected |
| FM service provision | The risk that the revenue received from the FM service is below that projected; the further risk of step-in |
| Interest rate risk | On all elements of the finance over the construction and contract periods; interest rate movements may also affect the investment value |
| Tax risk | Possible adverse changes to a range of taxes; corporate, VAT, stamp duty, and rating for example |
| Political risk | Possible adverse changes – it was not that long ago that political risk could directly lead to development land tax or rental capping |
| Contract risk | Default by various parties – the covenant strength of the various public sector bodies is not uniform; parties within a consortium may also default |

If the plan is particularly dated or the project particularly unique site identification may need to be more involved. It will still be necessary to have regard to current planning guidance. The site suitable for the development of the project need not be a greenfield site but may be a brownfield site. Furthermore, there may be an existing occupier and a more general employment allocation in the Local Plan. The key issue is the likelihood of a satisfactory planning permission being obtained.

Unfortunately one arm of government seeks to reduce the cost of government occupation and service provision, while another seeks to promote the use of brownfield land. There are obviously more risks associated with brownfield sites and development costs can be expected to be higher. On the basis of value for money or best value criteria a brownfield site will not often compare favourably with a greenfield site. A more holistic approach must be taken by government if they are to enhance the prospects of brownfield sites within the PFI. At present, unless a specific site is identified for the project, there is an in-built bias against brownfield sites. The RICS has been active in supporting research in the field of using private finance within urban regeneration. There is more scope for this to occur, and some government attempt to level the risk playing field would be welcome and is perhaps most likely to occur when the location of new PFI projects is analysed. Outside the education sector most have been built on greenfield sites. More comment on this issue is provided in Chapter 9.

Planning risk can be minimised if outline planning permission for the project is in place. Detailed permission cannot be obtained in the early stages in most projects, as the final design will not be known in sufficient detail. The public sector must also take care in the extent to which it drives the design. A public sector design concept may exist yet this should not prevent private sector innovation.

There are three principle aspects to planning risk. One is whether the planning permission will be obtained thus allowing the development to take place. The second risk is that of the time taken to obtain such permission, either by negotiation or on appeal. The third risk area is that of cost increases flowing from any planning condition or Section 106 agreement. Those with experience of the planning process will recognise that there is a wide variation in the performance of local authorities in terms of the time taken to reach a decision. The 'wish list' of items they will have in order for a permission to be released will also vary. Advice on the reasonableness of conditions or agreements can and should be sought in material cases.

Various sites will have different site conditions, not merely the presence or absence of contaminants but also differing geological conditions, which will lead to a variation in construction treatment and construction cost.

## Construction

The PFI will seek to place the construction risk with the bidder. There may be some limitation of the risk due to events outside the control of the parties; however, any limitation is likely to be limited. Any defects within the construction will need to be rectified by the bidder, an important point for those putting together a team to bid on a project. The contractor within the team will not want defects in the building to impact on the relationship with others in the consortium. Funding banks may require contract monitoring on their behalf to minimise likely problems during the operational phase. Defects will impact negatively on the investment value and in the ability of various parties to dispose of their interest in the project.

## Technical

There are a range of technical risks to be factored into the bid calculation. While the PFI seeks to encourage innovation, in a technical context there is a bias against the use of new products or procedures if these have not been thoroughly tested. The risk areas are not unrelated to each other and the construction and technical specification must work together. A bidder may build to a higher initial standard in the hope of reducing maintenance costs. Alternatively a lower build standard and technical specification may be used, reducing capital costs but increasing maintenance costs. Whichever approach is followed the minimum performance standards in the output specification should be noted. It is unlikely that the public sector would wish to see the minimum investment in capital terms.

## Revenue risk

The revenue risk is associated with all the areas in the contract which relate to payment. Payment may be reduced because public sector demand for the service decreases – this is a volume risk. There is an availability risk given the need to make a specified type and amount of accommodation available to a certain standard for occupation and use. Service standards may drop below prescribed levels and the payment stream may be affected through penalty clauses in the contract.

## Residual value risk

Residual value risk is essentially the risk that the value of the asset at the end of the contract period is different to that expected at the start. The initial assessment has to have regard to a future opinion of value and property expertise ought to be more widely called upon to determine such an assessment. In many projects the end value is arrived at by indexing costs against a standard. The index often reflects little of property market movements either in rental or capital terms. There is therefore a weakness in the system that property knowledge can exploit. For example, the residual value risk of a project in Reading and one in Ipswich may be equally weighted, and furthermore the likelihood of public sector demand altering may be the same. The public sector may be able to vacate a certain amount of accommodation, this then reverting to the bidder to let. However, the development viability of the project in Ipswich may be dependent on the public sector interest. The availability payment under the contract may exceed rental levels in that locality by some margin. Conversely the project in Reading may see an availability payment at levels below those of market rents. The vacant space arising in Reading could be expected to let easily at an attractive figure. The public sector reduction in demand may actually be a blessing rather than a vice. On the other hand in Ipswich the vacant space would incur a holding cost, could take a lot longer to relet and would affect the initial bid price adversely.

Little thought has been applied to the dynamics of property market economics in the PFI process in this particular area. Asking for break clauses in respect of accommodation having a market value in an attractive locality may not be met with great bidder hostility. Other project types, and projects in other areas could not hope to work on the basis of the same set of standard clauses and assumptions. The residual value risk is not always uniform, neither is the risk associated with the value of accommodation which may be vacated during the contract term.

## Service provision

The failure to provide services that lead to a loss in revenue has been noted in the context of revenue risk. The point is worthy of being restated. A step-in clause is almost certain to form part of the contract, and a total failure of service provision will impact on all areas of revenue income, not just the income from that service element. The nature of the FM service provider is one of the key factors in reaching a successful PFI conclusion. Treasury Taskforce Technical Note 3, *How to Appoint and Manage Advisers*, contains as Annex B a Tender Evaluation Table.[4] One of the criteria sought from the financial adviser is 'expertise in international capital markets, finance techniques and their impact on contract structure and negotiations'. This is fine in theory, but the practical financing of any PFI project will owe a lot to the bankability of the FM provider.

## Interest rate risk

This is perhaps self-explanatory – interest rates will impact upon both the cost of capital and service provision. Movements in interest rates may be hedged in the financing process if this is deemed advisable.

One lesser-known impact of interest rate risk relates to the movement of currency values. Certain projects may receive an element of grant aid and if this aid comes from Europe it is likely to be priced in ecus. In March 1999 a grant of 100,000 ecus would pay for more than the same grant three months later. The United Kingdom is yet to price internally in ecus therefore there is every prospect that the grant will be over or under that actually agreed when it is spent in pounds sterling.

## Tax risk

Tax risks can be broken down into two groups. The first group comprises tax changes that occur while a project is being developed. A different approach or course may be necessary to deal with the change which may increase the bid cost and cause delay within the project timetable. The point is similar to that for technical changes which may be introduced during the bid process, eg a change in Building Regulations. Other changes, which have caused problems during the bidding process include the FRS 5 (Financial Reporting Statement 5) issue discussed in more detail below.

Tax risks themselves that occur after project construction or operation comprise the second grouping. These tax risks will fall into three areas. The first is the introduction of a new tax or, albeit less likely, the removal of an existing tax. The second area relates to a change in the tax rate for a particular tax, eg the VAT rate on fuel payments being increased. The third grouping is an action that leads to a tax being paid. If a new area of building is constructed the rateable value of the project and consequently the rates paid will alter. If an area of accommodation is vacated there may be an empty property rates liability. Does the contract enable the owners of the space to strip it bare if it is not marketable in order to make the space incapable of beneficial occupation? If the space may still be needed or called upon by the public sector body even stripping it bare may not avoid a rating liability.

## Political risk

There is always a political risk with a contract that is to last for in the region of 30 years. The risk can be minimised but not eliminated. PFI/PPP projects are being explored in other countries where the political risk may well be different.

## Contract risk

Unfortunately parties do default on contracts, sometimes deliberately, sometimes through little or no fault of their own. The contract structure will attempt to cover all circumstances and. to provide a means by which the agreement operates. There is a risk that these provisions may be called upon. There is a further risk that a different legal interpretation may be put on the contract clause than that which the parties envisaged.

## Risk apportionment in projects to date

Risk apportionment has varied between the public and private sectors in projects signed to date. Some risks are also stated as having been shared; however, this risk-sharing can be weighted more in the direction of one party than the other. The relevant government department responsible for the project in question will provide some details of the arrangements which have been used in projects to date, though they are more likely to focus on the arrangements that they would *like* to see. Furthermore a number of locational or property risks, discussed earlier, may differ in a manner which has not been recognised by the public sector's financial advisers. The professional body often associated with quantifying and pricing risk, the Institute of Actuaries, is critical of the accountancy-based pricing of many risk areas.

The risks which should be transferred are those which offer value for money to transfer. The private sector will price all the risks which are placed upon it – too many risks priced too greatly and the project will not be affordable to the public sector. To complicate matters risk transfer is not merely about value for money or best value. Criteria may need to be met which necessitate the transfer of a certain amount of risk in given areas, regardless of the price of such a transfer. The contract structure test, for example, may need to be met by the transfer of a certain amount of risk.

The concept of the party best able to manage the risk has arisen. It is generally accepted that the risk should lie with the party best able to manage it. That is correct in theory but only if both parties quantify and price the risks in the same way. As discussed earlier a break clause on an accommodation project in Reading may be a blessing rather than a burden due to the strength of the occupational property market. The same would not be true for an occupational office project in Blackburn where the property market is just not as strong, nor is it likely to be in the foreseeable future.

To consider risk you need to consider the influence or the control you can exercise over an event and its impact: the probability of the event occurring both in whole or in part and the cost implications if it does occur.

In the Colfox School scheme Dorset County Council retained a number of the risks, including the volume of pupils attending the school, the delivery of core teaching responsibilities and the National Curriculum, and changes in legislation specifically affecting educational buildings, while linking the fee to the GDP Deflator covered general changes in prices. Fee linkage to the GDP Deflator is the stated aim of government in local authority projects. It has, for example, occurred in the Norfolk Constabulary scheme. However, there is more than one way to link to the GDP Deflator. (The GDP Deflator is an economic measure of a type similar to the Retail Prices Index.)

The Colfox scheme provides for a number of risks to be shared. These include certain matters relating to the residual value of the assets at the end of the contract period, the requirements for new capital expenditure as a result of new general legislation above a minimum level and the risk associated with certain *force majeure* events.

Risks transferred in the Colfox scheme include cost overruns in the design or construction of the assets, costs associated with any delay in connection with the completion of asset construction, the repair and replacement of assets including furniture and equipment, and the risk of obsolescence. The generation of a level of third-party income is also guaranteed.

The Edinburgh Royal Infirmary project transfers a number of risks via the payment mechanism. Volume risk is transferred in two categories, bed and non-bed space attendances, within a floor and ceiling figure. The building availability risk is transferred as is service performance risk. Other risks transferred include the risk of latent defects, considered so likely that the public sector comparator provided for an expected cost of £1.75 million and a net present value of £900,000. (The public sector comparator is defined in the Glossary.)

Other projects have seen risks shared to advantage. The Norfolk Constabulary HQ project, for example, saw the planning risk shared. The property advisers to the police obtained outline planning permission on the 11.05 acre site (4.47 hectares) together with consent for the communications mast. The bidder was left to obtain detailed permission for their particular scheme. Obtaining outline permission considerably reduced the planning risk to the private sector, the police being better placed to establish the consent in principal for the 60-metre high communications mast.

## Financial Reporting Statement 5 issues – the accountancy treatment debate

It is unfortunate that the question of accounting treatment has impacted so heavily on the PFI process, that impact resulting from the importance attached to the accounting treatment of a particular transaction. Often the accounting treatment has appeared more important than the substance of the transaction itself. This importance has been reflected in government guidance, which in turn has often been out of date soon after release as a result of debates about accounting methodology (see, for example, paragraph 2.11 of the September 1998 DETR explanatory note, *Local Government and The Private Finance Initiative*[7]).

We may now find that we have a position in which the accounting treatment of a project drives its very nature rather than recording accurately what actually exists. Following the first Bates Report, HM Treasury issued interim guidance on the accounting treatment of PFI transactions.[8] The Accounting Standards Board (ASB) issued a December 1997 Draft Amendment to FRS 5 which was intended to replace the interim guidance.[9] The ASB proposals resulted in much discussion in PFI circles, there were a number of speeches at conferences on the subject, and the debate made national broadsheet news. A number of consultation responses having been made, the final form of FRS 5 much resembled the original draft.[10] The subsequent Treasury guidance, rather than maintaining a different stance to the ASB, adopts the FRS as the basis on which projects must be recorded. (As noted earlier the basis of recording has tended to drive the structuring in the first place.)

FRS 5 defines an 'asset' as 'rights of access to future economic benefits controlled by an entity as a result of past transactions or events'. To avoid the total capital value of the project being taken on the PSBR in any one year, the government required PFI projects to be off balance sheet. It was therefore necessary for a PFI project to meet the FRS 5 test.

The Treasury appears to be a lot less worried about the new FRS 5 than was initially the case due to the proposed introduction of resource accounting.

The original position was to have PFI projects off balance sheet. Many early PFI and quasi-PFI schemes had a qualifying condition that they be off the public sector balance sheet. Compliance with the condition actually aided the PFI process from a bidder viewpoint. In general the condition could be met so an element of certainty was introduced to the process.

In introducing the revised FRS 5, Sir David Tweedie, ASB chairman, stated:

> What has worried many observers is the risk that assets and liabilities under PFI contracts end up on nobody's balance sheet. From an accounting viewpoint therefore, it is crucial to ensure that, where such a contract for services involves a substantial underlying property for its performance, that the property is recorded as an asset by whoever controls it, along with the liability to pay for it.

It is doubtful that the issue troubled as many observers as the ASB would have had people believe. Geoffrey Robinson, the then Paymaster-General, commented: 'Above all, PFI is driven by value for money and not by accounting treatment'. However, Mr Robinson may have been a little over-optimistic.

At the time of the draft amendment to FRS 5 the FRS 5 test was basically the question of whether or not there was an asset. If there was an asset it was necessary to reflect the asset on a balance sheet. Whether there was an asset was dependent upon how much the party bore the variations in profit and loss relating to the property and non-separable services. It was necessary to transfer 'ownership risks' to an extent that met the FRS 5 test for the project to be off balance sheet. The amount of 'ownership risk' and the nature of the risks themselves, to which the ASB document had regard, became the subject of representation from the property and construction sectors.

In the originally drafted ASB amendment it was considered possible to separate the asset and the service elements of a PFI contract. The document recognised an interrelationship between the service and capital elements in the context of a road project (paragraph F11), although it appeared not to recognise that the design of real estate may affect future maintenance. The point at issue was, to what extent could ownership risks be separated from the risks of operation and maintenance? The property and construction sectors were certainly confused. The ASB amendment was related to the balance sheet with the motivator of separating service and capital elements. The PFI was supposed to be an integrated one-stop shop to meet occupiers' requirements, the provision of a holistic product with an apparently seamless distinction between the physical being of the building and the service provided within. To meet the FRS 5 test it was necessary to meet a level of 'ownership risk transfer'. Arguments centred on what should constitute a risk for the purposes of transfer.

The FRS 5 test now recognises that the capital and service elements of a project may not always be separable. However, the main thrust is toward the original stance of separability. The practical point concerns the range of 'tests' capable of being used to determine the extent to which any party bears any variation in property profits or losses.

For those contracts that fall within the FRS we have noted that whether a party has an asset of the property is determined by looking at the extent to which each party would bear any variations in property profits or losses. The first principle – and the key to FRS 5 – is the separation of the contract. The document states that, 'any such separable elements that relate solely to services should be excluded when determining whether each party has an asset of the property.' The document continues by stating that because a contract designates payments as 'unitary' they should not be treated as such.

Paragraph F19 of FRS 5 provides the question for the asset test. (This will need to be read more than once!) It is necessary to look at the 'potential variations in costs and revenues that flow from features of the property – which are relevant to determining who has an asset of the property – from those that do not – and which are therefore not relevant to determining who has an asset of the property'.

Paragraph F22 of FRS 5 identifies a number of factors which may be relevant to the assessment of profit variation. These are as follows:

• demand risk;

- the presence or absence of third-party revenues;
- who determines the nature of the property;
- penalties for under-performance or non-availability;
- potential changes in relevant costs;
- obsolescence;
- the arrangements at the end of the contract and residual value risk.

It is worth us looking at some of these factors in a little more detail and also to consider areas in which property and construction thinking may differ from what the ASB have put in place. To be forewarned is to be forearmed.

### Demand risk

This refers to the uncertainty about the future level of demand for the property. The FRS talks about assessing the reality of the demand risk. The document states that there may be uncertainty over the demand for a certain property type in the long term. The document continues by stating that the purchaser (public sector) may fill the PFI property in preference to properties not subject to PFI. If this occurs and the PFI property is unlikely not to be full it is concluded that the purchaser has retained the demand risk. The PFI payments must vary with the demand or usage of the property, rather than the purchaser being obliged to pay for the output capacity, for the asset to be away from the purchaser.

FRS 5 states that, 'demand risk is imposed by the economic conditions of the market in which the PFI contract is written'. It is perhaps more correct to state that demand risk varies with the state of the market in the subject locality throughout the term of the contract and specifically prior to the contract signing and to any break points contained in the contract. The FRS talks about the reality of demand risk, but no thought is given to the magnitude of the risk. Consider two government office accommodation projects, one assumed to be in the Whitehall area of London and the other in Ipswich, with a further assumption that both projects are of a substantial size. On the same contract terms the demand risk would not be the same for the two projects. A bidder might be quite prepared to entertain large and frequent break clauses in the London accommodation, knowing that the space is likely to be able to be let at a good rent, one that may well exceed the original indexed-linked project pricing. On the other hand, the project in

Ipswich may not see a high level of demand, or demand at a level which is economically attractive when compared to the unitary charge in the PFI contract, should the government occupier vacate. There is a definite scope as presently drawn to play on demand risk issues. However, we face a fundamental problem when PFI projects are proposed for more disadvantaged areas or more economically challenging development sites where the degree of headline demand risk shift cannot be expected to be as great. To accept a small proportion of demand risk in certain projects may be equal to accepting a considerable amount in others (if the measure of demand risk shifting is simply how much of the accommodation can be handed back, how frequently and at what penalty).

## Third-party revenue

The FRS on this point is unlikely to cause great dissent or practical problems. Where an operator uses third-party revenue to cover property costs this is evidence of the property being an asset of the operator. If third-party usage is minimal or restricted, or if the purchaser guarantees the operator's income, it is stated that the property is more likely to be an asset of the purchaser. (Alternative revenue streams are discussed in more detail in Chapter 5.)

## Who determines the nature of the property

The FRS states that if the purchaser determines the key features of the property either by explicitly agreeing to them or through contractual acceptance at the end of the construction phase then there is a presumption that the purchaser has an asset. If the operator has significant discretion over how to fulfil the contract then this is an indication that the asset is with the operator. Construction risk is stated not to be generally relevant to determining which party has an asset, because 'such risk normally has no impact during the property's operational life'.

From a property and construction viewpoint the logic behind the above may seem to be among the weakest within the FRS. Construction risk can have quite a profound impact on the property during its anticipated life. Furthermore a contractual acceptance at the end of the construction phase does not in construction terms determine the nature of the property. It may recognise completion of construction but this is different to absolving the building of all defects.

## Penalties for under-performance or non-availability

This relates to penalties if the property is below a specified standard or is unavailable due to operator fault. The penalty should not be related purely to the services. Importance is attached to the likelihood of the penalty occurring so that if the operator has ample time to address the fault then the penalty may not be 'real'.

## Potential changes in relevant costs

The relevant costs under the terms of FRS 5 are property costs and not the cost of services. If property costs can be passed to the purchaser there is a presumption that the asset is that of the purchaser. If property costs are fixed or vary in relation to a general inflation index the presumption is toward the asset being that of the operator.

Viewed from a property perspective the above again distorts risk. Property has been seen as a hedge against inflation. However, rental growth is not uniform. In many areas and for many property types to grow the property cost at the RPI would be to exceed the growth rate in the market, while in other locations and sectors to have the growth at RPI would be to under-inflate compared to actual market movements. The Ipswich and London locations discussed earlier would illustrate the respective points. What this consideration actually does is interfere with the operation of any break clause. The purchaser of the London accommodation is highly unlikely to exercise any break, as alternative non-PFI rents are likely to be higher. With the Ipswich property the purchaser may have found that the property costs have grown (by reference to the RPI) at a rate which exceeds that elsewhere in the market. In this location a break is more likely to be exercised as the non-PFI property costs could well be cheaper.

For a greater appreciation of this point readers are recommended to consider a range of available material on rental growth in specific centres. One work which illustrates clearly how rental growth can differ in various locations is that by the present author looking at movements in rental levels between the 1995 and 2000 Rating Lists in respect of office property in the East Midlands and East Anglia, *Revaluation 2000: Office Property in the East Midlands and East Anglia*.[11]

## Obsolescence, including the effects of changes in technology

Where the potential for obsolescence is significant the party that bears the costs and benefits will be the one to whom the asset moves.

## The arrangements at the end of the contract/residual value risk

Residual value risk is the risk that the property at the end of the contract is different to that expected. The FRS states that, 'the price aspects of residual value risk cannot be reduced or increased by the contract. The contract can only influence those aspects of residual value risk relating to the condition of the property at the end of the contract.'

Unfortunately this does not seem to be the case and on this issue the ASB may well have shown a lack of appreciation as to the nature of built fixed assets. It is possible to maintain that the contract can facilitate or otherwise changes in the residual value. One example to illustrate the point is that of an operator who, in providing alternative revenue, creates a structure which has a value and is consequently something that would alter the residual value. A further example is the extent to which the contract imposes obligations on the occupier of any space that becomes surplus to the purchaser's needs.

## General note

As a general point in considering the FRS it is stated that the overall effect of all the above factors is to be taken into account in determining who has the asset. The comment to be made here is that the accounting treatment may well play a part in driving the nature of the asset and the liability rather than resulting in the true nature of assets and liabilities being recorded, while the argument remains that the separation of the asset and service elements remains too great and that 'risks' are not appropriately recognised.

## Chapter 8

# Partnerships UK

## Introduction

*Modern Government, Modern Procurement* is the title of an HM Treasury paper produced during July 1999.[12] The paper draws together two separate yet related studies of government procurement. The first of these is the Gershon Review looking at 'civil procurement in Central Government in the light of the Government's objectives on efficiency, modernisation and competitiveness in the short and medium term'.[13] The second work is the second Bates Review, which Sir Malcolm Bates was asked to undertake to follow his original review. The second Bates Review considers 'progress made by the Government in the delivery of PFI and PPPs and recommends changes to existing arrangements intended to improve further the Government's approach to PPPs'.[14]

The Treasury document noted above considers the key recommendations of the two reviews. The Gershon Review recommends the creation of the Office for Government Commerce within the Treasury. The Bates review identifies the continuing need for central expertise to assist the public sector and considers possible successors to the Treasury Taskforce.

The government's response to the second Bates Review was to announce the creation of Partnerships UK, itself to be established in the form of a Public Private Partnership.

## The second Bates Review

The Gershon Report talks of gateway-style reviews. To an extent these exist already in PFI as approval is required for a project before it can move beyond certain stages of the process. Bates talks about retaining the gateways that exist in PFI and of introducing them to other areas of the public sector. As Bates is implemented and evolves we are likely to see a range of gateways being introduced. At present these seem aimed at quality assurance and financial viability (or at least apparent financial appeal). We may also see some extension of the principle if government is to succeed in what it describes as 'joined up thinking'. There would be a clear ability to ensure that wider ranges of policy objectives are met at a gateway review.

Bates also discusses greater standardisation of the PFI process and of the contract terms. What is missing from the review in express terms is a desire to see standardised financial modelling. While it would not be possible to standardise all models or all the contract terms for various projects, the more the public sector can produce templates the shorter and less protracted the period leading to financial close will become.

Bates concludes that departmental private finance units continue to lack deal-making skills. The need for a body to provide central expertise remains. Bates identifies a number of other areas of weakness:

- strategic planning;
- project management;
- negotiating skills;
- financial disciplines; and
- the management of long-term contracts.

Bates discussed options for the provision of a central government source of expertise, one option being to establish a public private partnership to support public sector PFI procurement and PPPs with a combination of project and financial skills. Government considered the Bates Review and decided that the response would be the establishment of Partnerships UK.

## Partnerships UK

The stated aim of Partnerships UK is to deliver better value for money by working on the side of the public sector. At present Partnerships UK is not intended to be a bank as some commentators have suggested. The role is one that will require clarification over time, although it is stated that Partnerships UK will be able to provide development funding to get 'PFI deals off the ground, where existing forms of private finance are not available'. If Partnerships UK is in a position to provide some funding the commentator's confusion is understandable. There will also arise serious concerns over conflicts of interest. Partnerships UK will be advising one party yet providing finance to the 'opposite side', albeit in a partnership type project.

Partnerships UK is to operate in the private sector by making available to public sector procuring authorities the skills of individuals drawn from the private sector. It is intended that Partnerships UK will be a plc and that a majority interest will be held by the private sector. Government will be able to appoint a number of non-executive directors to represent its interests.

The new Office for Government Commerce will work in conjunction with Partnerships UK to support public sector procurement activity in certain areas. Although the Taskforce will continue to be responsible for PFI policy formulation and advice and the chairing of the Project Review Group, concern might be expressed about the access given to Partnerships UK.

The raising of private sector capital and the development of the business case for Partnerships UK is to take place during 1999 and the early part of 2000. It is expected that the raising of private sector capital will be tendered competitively.

What Partnerships UK really acknowledges are two factors apparent to most who have experience of PFI/PPP. The first is that public sector expertise may be weak, although this is not perhaps universally the case and it must be further noted that these parties tend to be advised by others. If public sector deal-concluding skills are weak the same comment can be applied to a number of solicitors and accountants who see it as their role to bring negotiations to a close. Lack of proper management of the advisers and the functions which they undertake is perhaps the greater weakness. The second factor, which the creation of Partnerships UK acknowledges, is the high cost of professional advice. If Partnerships UK reduces the cost to the public sector of the advice it receives then there will be a benefit to the greater good. If, however, public sector bodies are steered towards advice from Partnerships UK which is no more competitively priced, then departmental friction can be anticipated.

One problem to date is that PFI and PPP are seen as methods of procuring capital assets. They may be more than assets in that a service is provided, yet many are asset driven in the first instance. If you procure a building traditionally the role of the solicitor is well defined and often accountancy input is small. The professionals employed will be working at 1999 hourly rates of well below £100. The legal and accounting mix of the PFI is such that the role of these professionals has been expanded so that charging hourly fee rates of £200 to £300 is not uncommon. This can make PFI procurement an expensive business.

Standardisation of process and of a range of contract terms should improve the amount of money that can be saved in the procurement stage. Whether Partnerships UK with its private sector listing will achieve this is open to some debate. The capital base that is being considered for this organisation is such that many niche competitors will do well to compete effectively. Without true competition the anticipated savings may be less than anticipated.

## Chapter 9

# PFI and the planning process

An unpublished research report produced by the present author was referred to in *The Times*,[15] *The Estates Gazette*,[16] *Urban Environment Today*,[17] and *Planning Magazine*.[18] The report highlighted the amount of PFI development that was occurring on greenfield as opposed to brownfield sites. Those reading this who are bidders or contractors to projects may readily understand why this is the case. On the other hand, those considering the planning merits of a PFI scheme may not have the same initial understanding. This chapter seeks to explore the PFI process in a planning context and to provide those involved with a background understanding.

## Brownfield and greenfield sites

There are two groups of reasons why the PFI process favours greenfield over brownfield development. The first group relates to considerations of time. A public sector body procuring a project will have a target date for the commencement of its operation. If a bidder fails to meet this timescale they will be contractually penalised financially. Furthermore, if a bidder proposes a solution which is likely to overrun the deadline his bid is unlikely to become the preferred choice. A time pressure exists with most projects. There can be a delay in the department gaining approval for the scheme. The PFI selection process can be time consuming. There may be little time left after this to put a brownfield site in a development-ready condition.

With a brownfield site there are greater risks of finding more problems during the site investigation or construction phases. If these problems are likely to increase the development timescale bidders will have a natural preference for other sites.

The second group of reasons relates to the cost of development. It is almost invariably cheaper to build on a greenfield site than it is on a brownfield site. If it is cheaper to construct the facility on a greenfield site, then in so doing the bidder will be able to reduce the single unitary charge. Reducing the single unitary charge will also make the proposal more attractive to the public sector.

Earlier chapters have discussed the PFI evaluation process. It should be noted that site acceptability is one of the project selection considerations, acceptability both to the public sector body seeking to have the service provided and to the local planning authority. From the public sector client viewpoint, site acceptability will occur if the site falls within parameters set out in the *OJEC* notice. Site acceptability in a planning context arises if the site has outline planning permission or has an approved allocation in an adopted Local Plan.

The process is one which enables proposed sites to cross a threshold of acceptability. If a site is unlikely to receive planning permission then the site is likely to be considered unsuitable. Of all the sites that may be suitable a planning authority may have an order of development preference. While this order may place brownfield sites above greenfield sites, there is at present little incentive for brownfield sites to be developed first.

One good example of a PFI project occurring on a brownfield site is the new Hereford Hospital. The planners in Hereford positively resisted greenfield development and steered the NHS trust to the brownfield site. In the case of projects such as the Cumbria Police scheme at Workington the original *OJEC* notice specified a location for the project within 1 km of Workington town centre, the police having undertaken a full options study and locational analysis to decide on the optimum location for the development. This location falls within an area which lends itself to brownfield rather than greenfield development. However, the planning problems at Workington following initial site selection illustrate the risks that remain in the PFI process. Planning officers and their elected members may not always be of like mind.

The Workington project assists urban development due to the location specified in the *OJEC* notice. If a wider area is specified this could include greenfield sites, and if an allocated greenfield site is promoted planning permission may be difficult to refuse. On the other hand, a project which occurs on a greenfield site may bring benefits, yet the wider benefits may be greater if the project can be brought forward on a brownfield site. On the other hand the development costs of a brownfield site are almost invariably higher than those of a greenfield equivalent, and if the development costs are higher the single unitary charge is also likely to be higher. Thus the wider public good which the planners may be seeking through a brownfield development may have a public cost borne by the public sector body in question paying a higher single unitary charge.

Generally PFI projects are viewed only from the perspective of the central government department promoting them and any wider social benefits which may arise from the project may be excluded from the decision-making process. However, it is also true to say there is a problem with finding a mechanism to assess these wider benefits. The public sector body will tend to be constrained with regard to the bid selection factors which they can consider by advice from their lawyers on that which it is permissible to consider.

The public sector body promoting the project specifies the general location of the project (the statement made in the *OJEC* notice). There are therefore limits on the influence of the local planning authority unless the local authority promotes the project itself, eg the Leyton School scheme promoted by Waltham Forest Borough Council. Here the planning authority worked with the education authority to identify a suitable project site. There are a large number of opportunities which local authorities can seize using the PFI and PPP to procure projects that in turn have wider social benefits. Other local interest groups can become a party to the process, provided that the decision-making process itself does not become too fragmented. Streamlining the decision-making process in respect of local authority projects is key to their timely success. Key staff must be appointed to a role and trusted to undertake the same. Democratic accountability must take place at key identified stages.

Those public sector bodies wishing to promote a successful project may wish to ensure that a range of sites can be developed to meet the output specification. A choice of sites will lead to a range of development costs, and with a range of costs there is by definition a lowest cost. Those planning authorities concerned about Local Plan development land allocations may wish to try and influence the content of any *OJEC* notice, thus acting as a preliminary steerage to project location. Subsequent discussions may focus heavily on development economics. These matters translate directly to 'best value' concerns for the sponsoring public sector body.

One consideration of the PFI process is that the party best able to manage a particular risk be responsible for that risk. In a planning context this has tended to involve the public sector body obtaining an outline planning permission and the private sector partner obtaining the subsequent detailed permission. While this is not always the case, it is strongly recommended that consideration be given as to how the planning process may best be handled. A fire brigade or police authority coming forward with an outline application for a communications mast is likely to be treated more favourably than a private sector concern which has less evidence to offer to justify the height of the mast proposed. Similarly there may be scope for mitigating the conditions which are imposed on a planning permission or the provisions that may be sought under a Section 106 agreement.

## The planning application process

The statutory period for a planning authority to determine an application is eight weeks after the date of registration though few planning authorities keep to this timescale in respect of major commercial projects. Those planning a project flow chart should not assume that a decision would be received within the eight-week time period. In fact the planning authority may decide to consult in a wider fashion; for example, with the Norfolk Constabulary Headquarters, Communications and Operations Centre project the planning authority, South Norfolk District Council, even sought comment on the design from the Royal Fine Arts Commission.

After expiry of the eight-week time period a non-determination appeal may be made to the Secretary of State via the Planning Inspectorate in Bristol. The parties should agree when any non-determination appeal should be made, if at all. An eight-week period may be too soon to realistically expect a decision. The view of the planning authority at this time may, however, help gauge the future strategy. There is always the option of making two applications, appealing one and leaving the other for the authority to determine, although this strategy is unlikely to be suited to many PFI projects. Those making applications are encouraged to monitor closely the progress and viewpoint of the planning authority. The contract between the parties should provide for the outcome of all planning matters which are not addressed at the time the contract is signed. This should include who has the right to force an appeal and at what point in time. It may also be necessary to refer to the costs of any appeal – these are an issue of risk transfer discussed in Chapter 7.

The agreement should further ensure that any building is built in accordance with the planning permission granted and that all conditions are met and complied with. It may in certain circumstances be thought advisable for the parties to appeal against planning conditions that are deemed unsatisfactory. The contract should provide a mechanism for addressing this in respect of any planning conditions that are not known about at the date of the contract.

## Chapter 10

# Valuation issues

## Rating

Rates are a tax on the occupation of property. Although the unitary charge may refer to one single payment for the occupation of the property and the services provided, it is highly likely that in most cases the rates payable will be borne by the occupier, the public sector body seeking the service provision.

Rates are also paid on empty property. At the time of writing industrial property benefits from a system that does not charge when industrial property is empty. Commercial property, such as an office building, has a payment regime which provides that no charge is made for the first three months of the property becoming vacant. Thereafter, rates are paid at a level of 50 per cent of the full charge. (Unless the property is a Listed Building or was last occupied by a charity).

When looking at a rating issue the nature and description of the property is all-important. The first consideration is that of 'what makes up the hereditament?' The hereditament can be described as the area of property upon which a rateable value is set. In turn from a rateable value you arrive at the rates payable by multiplying the rateable value with the uniform business rate and factoring in any transitional or other alterations introduced by central government. The hereditament is important in considering whether the property is occupied or not. If the entire hereditament is occupied rates will be paid in full on the whole property. For example, consider a four-storey office building, all the floors of which are occupied by one concern. This is likely to constitute one hereditament with one rateable value. If the company vacates one floor and there is still one hereditament, they will continue to pay rates as if the whole where occupied. In order that the one vacant floor benefits from empty rate provisions it will need to have its own separate rateable value, and to be capable of having a separate rateable value it must be capable of meeting a number of tests. Broadly speaking these tests are those which prove that the accommodation is vacant and to let, and that it could physically be occupied by another party.

In general the design of the building and the arrangement of the accommodation will have to allow for genuine subdivision if hereditaments are to be capable of being split to reflect vacant accommodation.

The above discussion noted that empty property is treated more favourably than occupied property in terms of the sums of money actually paid in tax. Upon accommodation becoming vacant it was noted that there is (as the system stands at present) a three-month payment holiday for all types of accommodation. This holiday only occurs once in a relatively short space of time. Therefore, if the public sector body in a PFI contract occupies space in a building and then decides that 20 per cent of that space will be vacated, the contract will need to determine who has the liability to pay the rates on the 20 per cent of the accommodation vacated. In strict terms if the accommodation is vacated by a break clause being exercised then the liability to pay the rates will revert to the owner (the service supplier). If the public sector body winds down the use of that accommodation early and vacates the same prior to the actual date of vacation in the break clause it may benefit from the three-month rate holiday. If all of this period has been used by the time the accommodation reverts to the supplier, the supplier will not benefit from another three-month period. Again, the contract may attempt to deal with this point, and is one of the reasons why a 'keep open' or 'keep trading clause' may be inserted into a lease.

The field of rating is complex and there are special provisions that apply to charities, listed buildings and a number of other property types, and to types of property occupier. With any project both parties are advised to consult with a suitably qualified chartered surveyor, preferably one with knowledge of PFI and rating.

One other practical point about the nature of a hereditament which those who are party to a contract should be aware of and provide for is the question of accommodation used solely by the service provider – a help desk, management and maintenance office, for example. It may be that this area gives rise to a separate hereditament. If the conditions of rateable occupation are met, the service providers may find themselves receiving a rates bill based on a rateable value for this area.

So a separate hereditament gives rise to a separate rateable value, but what exactly is a rateable value and how is it calculated? The statutory definition of a rateable value is contained within paragraph 2, Schedule 6, of the Local Government Finance Act 1988. It reads as follows:

> The rateable value of a non-domestic hereditament shall be taken to be
> an amount equal to the rent which it is estimated the hereditament
> might reasonably be expected to let from year to year if the tenant
> undertook to pay all usual tenant's rates and taxes and to bear the cost
> of any repairs and insurance and the other expenses (if any) necessary
> to maintain the hereditament in a state to command that rent.

From the above it can be seen that a rateable value amounts to a
rental value given certain assumptions. A rental value under the
terms of a lease may not be the same as a rateable value – they may
have different valuation assumptions. However, a surveyor should
be able to relate one to the other, and the rental value under a lease
may be used in evidence at a tribunal hearing to deal with a dispute
as to the level of rateable value. With many common property types
the valuation approach to assessing a rateable value is to calculate
from comparable rental transactions the appropriate figure,
adjustments being made to put the rental transaction on the same
basis as the statutory definition.

A rent under a lease may have a bearing on the rateable value
and consequently the rates paid. However, all of the service
provision will need to be stripped away from the calculation. A
strange result may occur if the payment for the PFI accommodation
is widely different in rental terms to similar rented accommodation
in the area.

The following is an example of how a rateable value might be
arrived at for an office building. This could be an office building
procured using the PFI.

Each area of the property is taken and an appropriate rate per
square metre is applied to each of the areas. The rate per square
metre is used to represent the rateable value of the space as defined
by statute and is really equivalent to the rental value of the area on
the given assumptions. Additions will be made for factors like air-
conditioning while a number of deductions may be made to reflect
other valuation adjustments. A rate will be applied to each of the
car parking spaces. A simple rating valuation on this basis may be
as follows:

| | |
|---|---:|
| 1,000 square metres of office space at £90 per square metre | £90,000 |
| 500 square metres air-conditioned office space at £100 per square metre | £50,000 |
| 300 square metres of stores at £45 per square metre | £13,500 |
| 100 car parking spaces each at £250 | £25,000 |

Adding together the above gives the base rateable value of £178,500. There may then be a number of end allowances to be made to reflect, for example, the location or arrangement of the building. The rateable value will then be multiplied by the uniform business rate to produce the rates payable. While there may be transitional adjustments to be factored in, this is the basic calculation.

With a number of more specialised or unusual properties, a different valuation basis may be used to calculate the rateable value. One such approach that may be applied to a number of PFI or PPP projects is the Contractor's Test. A rental value is derived for the accommodation from a depreciated replacement cost of the same. This approach has been used for many theatres and concert halls and can become quite complex when arguments that the project only occurred because of grant subsidy are entered into the equation. For a number of PFI and PPP projects assessed on a Contractor's Test basis there will be disappointment at the seemingly high level of rateable value set and arguments can be anticipated that the project only occurred because of a PFI or PPP contract arrangement.

The Contractor's Test is also used to calculate the rateable value for many property types that are subject to PFI transactions, for example schools and hospitals. The capital cost of the building is decapitalised using a decapitalisation rate to provide an annual rateable value. Construction costs have risen over recent years and it had been expected in rating circles that the decapitalisation rate would be reduced. However, the latest consultation in advance of the Year 2000 Rating Revaluation proposes leaving the decapitalisation rate at the same level as the 1995 Revaluation. If the decapitalisation rate is left the same occupiers of buildings assessed on such a basis are likely to see a large headline increase in rateable value and consequently rates paid.

## Capital valuation of the PFI project

Various parties may have an interest in the project that requires a capital valuation. Furthermore, financing banks may require a valuation for loan security purposes. Each of these valuations poses difficulties for those entrusted with the task.

### *A valuation for loan security*

The financing banks will be lending to the preferred bidder and the team of service suppliers. The security will be the contract between the supplier and the public sector body. The income will be the single unitary charge as it is anticipated to occur throughout the contract period. Instructions will need to be sought about the extent to which it is the property income as distinct from the service income which is being valued. However, the distinction is artificial when service standards are not met and the contract stipulates there is no property income. The level of property income throughout the term of the contract is therefore in part dependent upon the parties to that contract. A strong service provider with a good track record and good covenant strength may find it easier to secure finance at more competitive rates when compared to service providers of weaker standing.

The amount and timing of any break clauses will also affect the valuation, as will the likelihood of those break clauses being exercised. When considering various risks it was pointed out that indexing payments to an indicator such as the GDP Deflator might make the property comparatively cheap, or comparatively expensive, when compared with rental accommodation available in the local property market. This comparative exercise may in future years need to be undertaken as part of the process of anticipating whether the exercise of a break clause is likely. If the break clause is exercised what is then likely to be the income from the property?

A discounted cash flow approach will probably be necessary to consider the various payments received and spent and also to provide a basis for considering various scenarios regarding how the contract actually operates.

Unfortunately, as at the end of 1999, *The RICS Appraisal and Valuation Manual*[19] offers little specific assistance with regard to the valuing of PFI projects. The RICS PFI Policy Panel has asked that issues arising be considered, and the response is awaited.

## Formal asset valuation

It is likely that the asset will revert to the public sector after the expiry of the contract period. Although in a number of PFI projects the asset remains with the private sector, it is becoming more usual for the public sector to be left with the asset. Variations can be expected as to who is left with the asset at the end of the contract period, or some agreed extension of the contract period. However, an assessment will need to be made as to the value of this interest. In property terms this is difficult because an estimated rental value will need to be applied to the property at a point in the future, with a capital value then derived from this. The property itself may alter, and alternative revenue proposals may lead to the building of structures which themselves add a value when the contract expires.

Prior to the asset reverting there will be a number of interests that could be valued on behalf of both the public and private sectors. These interests need to be considered in the context of the wider PFI contract. While a lease may be in place it is not necessarily just the asset or liability of the lease which is being valued – it is the arrangement which this document has with the other PFI contract paperwork. This paperwork will determine when, and by whom, various areas of the accommodation are refitted or service provision is upgraded.

The asset may need to appear on the balance sheet of one or more of the parties, and how this asset appears is likely to be one of the key questions in forthcoming years. If there is a market in the equity within PFI projects the valuation approach may in part be equity driven. There will, however, still be a need for the artificial split to create the value of the property element required by accounting standards. To relate fairly to other real estate holdings in the area the property element of the PFI project must compare realistically with these other assets. This may result in certain projects having an underlying property value which appears high, while other projects have a property asset value that appears low.

## Chapter 11

# The interrelationship between the PFI, statute and other fields of knowledge

## Introduction

The chapters of this book relating to town and country planning and valuation issues illustrate two areas in which PFI projects operate in a controlled environment where the PFI project is subject to wider statutory process and regulation. The purpose of this chapter is to comment on other areas in which the PFI process is affected by wider legislation. This chapter does not contain a definitive listing of all such topics, but provides a brief practical guide to some of the more relevant issues facing property and construction.

## The Housing Grants, Construction and Regeneration Act 1996

All UK civil engineering and construction contracts entered into after 1 May 1998 are governed by Part II of the Housing Grants, Construction and Regeneration Act 1996. Construction contracts are defined in Section 104 of the Act, commonly known as the Construction Act.[20] The definition of what is a construction contract is wide and can cover many maintenance contracts and professional engagements. An exclusion order and regulations also exist omitting certain contracts from the effects of the Act.[21] One contract type, which is specifically excluded, is agreements entered into by specified public bodies under the Private Finance Initiative.

If the Act applied to PFI schemes the imposition of a stage payment mechanism, as required by the Act, would make the financing of a PFI transaction extremely difficult, if not impossible. While the Act does exclude the PFI project agreement from compliance, it does not exclude works which the private sector provider subcontracts to another party. This may lead to the situation where the actual contract to construct the facility made between the private sector provider and a contractor is subject to the adjudication provisions of the Act whereas the project agreement, which sits above, made between the awarding authority and the private sector provider is not subject to those same provisions.

Until this state of affairs is further clarified all parties involved in the construction of a PFI project should be aware of the situation and protect their position accordingly in the contract or the project agreement.

## TUPE

The Transfer of Undertakings (Protection of Employment) Regulations[22] have caused many solicitors involved within PFI contracts some difficulty. The effect of the regulations is becoming more clearly established following a number of cases in the House of Lords. The application of the regulations is a legal question. In any given project the awarding authority should be able to state to what extent individuals are affected. The applicability of the regulations should be decided on in every case. The practical issue for the property professional is akin to that of a client purchasing a trading business such as a hotel. If there are to be redundancies, the costs of these, and their fairness, may be an issue for the private sector provider.

## The CDM Regulations

A construction project forming part of a PFI contract will still be subject to the provisions of the Construction (Design and Management) Regulations 1994[23] which impose statutory duties on clients, designers, planning supervisors and contractors. The legislation covers pre-contract planning and relates to all stages of a construction project from the feasibility stage. There is a strong argument that the awarding authority should have in place a competent planning supervisor until such time as the contractor takes over the principal duties. The public sector body may still be the 'client' and may still require its position to be protected. The project agreement should allow for compliance with the legislation and enable those responsible for health and safety to undertake the role in a satisfactory manner.

It is recommended that all public sector bodies clarify with their legal advisers that the requirements of the legislation as it applies to them are being met. The awarding authority should in turn ensure that the private sector provider meets with the obligations imposed by the regulations.

# Government departmental PFI units

*Agriculture*
William Arnott
Head of Financial Policy Division
Ministry of Agriculture, Fisheries
and Food
Room 311
Whitehall Place (West Block)
London
SW1A2HH

Tel 020 7270 8423
Fax 020 7270 8436

*Culture, Media and Sport*
John Kempsell
Finance Division
Department for Culture,
Media and Sport
2–4 Cockspur Street
London
SW1Y 5DH

Tel 020 7211 6217
Fax 020 7211 6227

*Customs and Excise*
John Evans
Private Finance Unit
HM Customs and Excise
New King's Beam House
22 Upper Ground
London
SE1 9PJ

Tel 020 7865 5748
Fax 020 7865 5700

*Defence*
Peter Ryan
Head of Public Private
Partnership Unit
Ministry of Defence
Room G8, Metropole Building
Northumberland Avenue
London WC2N 5BL

Tel 020 7218 0983
Fax 020 7218 0055

*Education and Employment*
Stephen Burt
Head of Private Finance Division
Department for Education
and Employment
Room 510
Sanctuary Buildings
Great Smith Street
London SW1P 3BT

Tel 020 7925 6087
Fax 020 7925 5113

*Education and Employment (Schools)*
Richard Wilkinson
Department of Education
and Employment
Room 3.09
Sanctuary Buildings
Great Smith Street
London SW1P 3BT

Tel 020 7925 6566
Fax 020 7925 6987

*Environment Transport and the
Regions*
Crispin Tuckley
Department of Environment
Transport and the Regions
Private Finance Unit
Ashdown House
123 Victoria Street
London
SW1E 6DE

Tel 020 7890 5014
Fax 020 7890 5009

*Foreign and Commonwealth Office*
Martin Williamson
Head of Resource Planning
Foreign & Commonwealth Office
Room 4.2.16
1 Palace Street
London SW1E 5HE

Tel 020 7238 4016
Fax 020 7238 4004

*Health*
Peter Coates
Private Finance Unit
NHS Executive
Department of Health
Quarry House
Quarry Hill
Leeds LS2 7UE

Tel 0113 2545 487
Fax 0113 2545 406

*In London:*
Department of Health PFU
Room 363C, Skipton House
80 London Road
London
SE1 6LW

Tel 020 7972 1694
Fax 020 7972 1697

*Home Office*
Polly Leithead
Home Office Procurement Unit
Room 965B
50 Queen Anne's Gate
London
SW1H 9AT

Tel 020 7273 3480
Fax 020 7273 2404

*Inland Revenue*
Jerry Page
Private Finance Unit
Inland Revenue
Somerset House
Strand
London
WC2R 1LB

Tel 020 7438 7294
Fax 020 7438 7663

*International Development*
Graham Stegmann
Principal Finance Officer
94 Victoria Street
London
SW1E 5JL

Tel 020 7917 0407
Fax 020 7917 0694

*Lord Chancellor's Department*
Richard Atkinson
PFI Unit
Lord Chancellor's Department
Room 923
Selborne House
54–60 Victoria Street
London
SW1E 6QW

Tel 020 7210 8631
Fax 020 7210 8577

*Northern Ireland Civil Service*
James McAleer
Department of Finance
Rathgael House
Balloo Road
Bangor
BT19 7NA
Tel 01247 858187
Fax 01247 858202

*Public Service*
Pat Pattenden
Cabinet Office
Procurement Policy Unit
Room 407
Queen Anne's Chambers
28 Broadway
London
SW1H 9JS
Tel 020 7210 0578
Fax 020 7210 0591

*Trade and Industry*
David Fincham
PFI Unit
Management Directorate
Department of Trade and Industry
Room 3.H.18
1 Victoria Street
London SW1H 0ET
Tel 020 7215 6832
Fax 020 7215 6739

*Scottish Office*
John Henderson
Head of the Private Finance Unit
Scottish Office
3–C25 Victoria Quay
Edinburgh
EH6 6QQ
Tel 0131 244 7497
Fax 0131 244 7499

*Social Security*
Sue Joseph
Head of Corporate PFI
Supply Management Group
Department of Social Security
Room 547, New Court
Carey Street
London
WC2A2LS
Tel 020 7412 1405
Fax 020 7412 1398

*Welsh Office*
Laurie Pavelin
Private Finance Unit
National Assembly for Wales
Government Buildings
Cathay's Park
Cardiff CF1 3NQ
Tel 02920 823383
Fax 02920 825390

# Glossary of PFI terms

**Affordability**. The privately funded scheme has to be affordable. The NPV of the project may need to be below a given figure (and definitely below the PSC, without good reason to depart from this); the payments under the contract must also be affordable. The private sector would wish to see an indication of the affordability threshold for a project. But for the public sector this is akin to stating how much they have to spend. At some point in the bidder selection process affordability levels are likely to be clarified; this is unlikely to be at the start of the process.

**Alternative revenue streams**. Ideas for third-party income that can arise from the project or because of the project. The third-party income is likely to be split in an agreed fashion between the bidder and the public sector client. The client may benefit from alternative revenue streams as they can be applied to reduce the single unitary charge and consequently make the project more affordable. If the bidder can assist in making the project more affordable and in reducing the single unitary charge he will be increasing dramatically the chances of his bid being successful.

**The authority**. The term given to the public sector body which is awarding the contract. This may, for example, be the Lord Chancellor's Department or a particular NHS Trust.

**BAFO (best and final offers)**. A stage in the PFI selection process. Discussed in more detail in Chapter 3.

**Benchmarking**. Services will have a cost to the public sector. The private sector may be asked to market test these at intervals or to benchmark the cost of service provision against an agreed basket of comparables.

**Best value**. A standard placed on certain public sector bodies regarding how they procure services. Best value is an extension of the concept of value for money.

**Bidder**. Generally considered as the party bidding for a PFI contract. This may be one company or organisation or a grouping of a number of such bodies. Consortia are becoming increasingly common and links are being established between organisations to work on different types of project in different market sectors. The client is usually seen as the public sector body procuring the service.

**Facilities management.** The term given to the process of managing the building and the services provided within it during the life of the building or for the duration of a contract.

**Financial model.** All PFI projects will need to be evaluated for a range of reasons, including that of bid selection. One important tool is the financial model. It shows the costs and revenues anticipated from the project, areas where there may be excess profits being made and areas where cost savings could be introduced.

**GDP Deflator.** The GDP Deflator is derived implicitly by dividing GDP at current prices by GDP at constant prices expressed in index form (GDP stands for Gross Domestic Product):

$$UK_{GDP} \quad = \quad UK_A + UK_{XT} - UK_{IT}$$

where:

| | | |
|---|---|---|
| $UK_A$ | = | real domestic absorption; |
| $UK_{XT}$ | = | total exports volume; |
| $UK_{IT}$ | = | total imports volume. |

Real domestic absorption is itself as follows:

$$UK_A \quad = UK_C + UK_{Invest} + UK_G$$

where:

| | |
|---|---|
| $UK_C$ | = real household expenditure; |
| $UK_{Invest}$ | = real gross business investment; |
| $UK_G$ | = real government spending on goods and services. |

**ITN (invitation to negotiate).** A stage in the PFI process. Discussed in detail and context in Chapter 3 of this book.

**ISOP (invitation to submit outline proposals).** One of the earlier stages of the bid evaluation process discussed in detail in Chapters 3 and 4.

**ITT (invitation to tender).** A further key stage in the PFI process. Discussed more fully in Chapter 3.

**Market testing.** A reference to obtaining comparable prices for a given function, service or cost item. The idea of market testing is to ensure best value.

*OJEC* **(The Official Journal of the European Communities).** Publication in which all project notices (tenders) appear. *OJEC* is published in electronic form over the Internet. Some sites containing *OJEC* notices charge for access, other sites are free. The Treasury Taskforce website is free to access and provides current notices. *OJEC* notices will stipulate the date by which a response is required to the advertisement. The deadlines stipulated in *OJEC* notices are strict and should be adhered to. *OJEC* will also contain prior information notices, which provide details about forthcoming projects.

**PIM (pre-qualification information memorandum)**. A document that sets out the nature and scope of the project as defined by the public sector body. The document is usually sent in response to an initial expression of interest. The document may contain a confidentiality requirement and will also contain caveats on behalf of the public sector team regarding its content.

**PSP (private sector provider)**. This is the party who actually comes through the selection process. The party nominated as preferred bidder who then proceeds to reach financial close and then project implementation.

**Public Sector Comparator (PSC)**. All projects are to have a PSC which is used to measure the privately funded alternative in terms of value for money or best value. The nature of what the PSC is for a given project can provoke debate. The private sector would like to know the actual cost of the PSC in NPV (net present value) terms. The public sector may not wish to release the NPV, at least in the initial stages of bidder selection. In all cases the private sector should understand how the PSC has been calculated. The same factors should apply as with the PFI project in order to compare like with like. In certain cases the PSC may be notional as there might not actually be a publicly funded alternative capable of occurring.

**RFQ (request for qualification)**. Essentially this is the response to the initial questionnaire submitted in an attempt to qualify for the 'long list' stage of the selection process.

**Risk**. There are a number of risks associated with a PFI project, the nature of which is discussed more fully in Chapter 7. A risk in itself arises when there is the possibility of more than one outcome to a given situation, and all outcomes are not deemed equal in the bearing they have on the project.

**Risk matrix**. A table which identifies all of the risks thought to be present and which shows the extent that each party will be exposed to those risks. A risk matrix is a useful tool in bid selection and evaluation, and also in attempting to establish whether various requirements for risk transfer have been met.

**Risk transfer**. For reasons that are explored in the text risk transfer needs to occur in PFI projects. The concept is the passing of various risks from the public sector to the private sector. While a degree of risk transfer will need to take place for a PFI project to occur, there has been a tendency for the public sector to attempt to pass all the risks associated with the project to the private sector. The private sector will price all such risks transferred and consequently transferring all risks may not offer the best value as the price is likely to increase. As a result the concept of having the risks with the party best able to manage them has arisen.

**Services**. Those items which the supplier is contracted to provide within the facility (or elsewhere). Services may be grouped in a number of different ways, eg hard and soft services. Payments for service provision are discussed in more detail in Chapter 6 which also provides definitions relating to various types of service payment. There will be a need to structure PFI contracts to ensure that service payments can vary with usage and performance.

**Service provider.** This may be the one party under the contract charged to provide all the services sought by the public sector body, or it may be each of the service providers themselves who perform a service function.

**Single unitary charge.** The private sector constructs the building and operates the service for which it will be paid a single unitary charge, the theory being that the public sector should make just one payment for their occupation. Rating law has yet to fit in with government decrees on the single unitary charge and consequently the public sector body is likely to be paying the charge and business rates, which are a tax on the occupation of property. More comment is provided on property issues in Chapters 7 and 10.

**Special purpose vehicle.** The preferred bidder will usually provide the service through a separate legal entity created for the purpose of the PFI project which will take the form of a special purpose vehicle. This vehicle may be formed as a separate company, as a limited liability partnership, or in some other manner. The basis of formation will attempt to offer the best tax regime for the bidder. Certain public sector bodies should be aware that some special purpose vehicles might wish to base themselves offshore. Bidders should be careful not to unduly offer the potential to embarrass government in the conduct of their affairs.

**TUPE.** The application of the Transfer of Undertakings (Protection of Employment) Regulations to PFI and PPP transactions. The regulations apply when there is a transfer of a qualifying undertaking. Parties to a PFI contract should consult with their legal advisers to see who may be affected by TUPE and the bearing this then has on the project.

**Value for money.** In simple terms this occurs when the privately funded project has a lower NPV than the PSC. However, the NPV may not be the only factor of a financial nature which is considered: the actual timing of the payments over the contract period may impact on the public sector value for money equation. Best value is an extension and slight redefinition of the value for money concept. In theory best value may take a more holistic approach to the provision of groups of services.

# Bibliography

1 Sir Malcolm Bates, *The first report on the Private Finance Initiative*, for HM Government, June 1997. . . . . . . . . . . . . . . . . . . . . . . . . . . . . . 2

2 The Treasury Committee, *The Private Finance Initiative. The Government's response to the 6th Report*. London: HMSO, 1996 . . . . . . . 2

3 The PFI Policy Panel of the The Royal Institution of Chartered Surveyors, *Private Finance Initiative: AGuidance Note*. RICS Books, September 1998. . . . . . . . . . . . . . . . . . . . . . . . . . . . . . . 16

4 Treasury Taskforce, *How to Appoint and Manage Advisers to PFI projects*, Technical Note 3. London: Treasury Taskforce: August 1998 . . . . . . . . . . . . . . . . . . . . . . . . . . . . . . . . . 16, 26, 51

5 Home Office CBSU Architectural Research and Advisory Group, *Police Buildings Design Guide*, vols I and II. London: Home Office, 1994 . . . . . . . . . . . . . . . . . . . . . . . . . . . . . . . . . . . . 30, 32

6 'Letters to the Editor', *The Independent*, 20th July 1999. . . . . . . . . . . . 39

7 Department of the Environment Transport and the Regions, *Local Government and The Private Finance Initiative*. London: DETR, 1998. . . . . . . . . . . . . . . . . . . . . . . . . . . . . . . . . . . . . . . . 55

8 HM Treasury, *Interim Guidance on the Accounting Treatment of PFI Transactions*. London: HM Treasury, 1997 . . . . . . . . . . . . . . . . . 55

9 Accounting Standards Board, *Draft Amendment to FRS 5*. London: ASB, 1997. . . . . . . . . . . . . . . . . . . . . . . . . . . . . . . . . . . . 55

10 Accounting Standards Board, *Amendment to FRS 5*. London: ASB, 1998 . . . . . . . . . . . . . . . . . . . . . . . . . . . . . . . . . . . . . . . 55

11 M. Blackwell, Revaluation 2000: *Office property in the East Midlands and East Anglia*. Rocklobster Publishing/Lance Publishing, 1998 (available from RICS Books (tel 020 7222 7000)). . . . . . . . . . . . . . . . . . . . . . . . . . . . . . . . . . . . 60

12 HM Treasury, *Modern Government, Modern Procurement*. London: HM Treasury 1999. . . . . . . . . . . . . . . . . . . . . . . . . . . . . . 63

13 Peter Gershon, *Civil Procurement in Central Government in the Light of the Government's Objectives on Efficiency, Modernisation and Competitiveness in the Short and Medium Term*. A review for HM Government commissioned autumn 1998, released 1999. . . . . . 63

14 Sir Malcolm Bates, *Second review of the Private Finance Initiative*, for HM Government released 1999. Summary recommendations 19 March 1999. . . . . . . . . . . . . . . . . . . . . . . . . . . . . . . . . . . . . . 63

15 *The Times*, 4 August 1999, p. 32. . . . . . . . . . . . . . . . . . . . . . . . . . . . 67

16 *Estates Gazette*, 24 July 1999, p. 30. . . . . . . . . . . . . . . . . . . . . . . . . . . . . . 67

17 *Urban Environment Today*, no. 77, 19 August 1999, p. 2. . . . . . . . . . . . 67

18 *Planning Magazine: The Journal of the Royal Town Planning Institute*, 20 August 1999, p. 12; see also the issue of 13 August . . . . 67

19 Royal Institution of Chartered Surveyors, *Appraisal and Valuation Manual*. RICS, updated regularly . . . . . . . . . . . . . . . . . . . . . 77

20 The Housing Grants, Construction and Regeneration Act 1996, available from the Stationery Office, London. For further guidance on the Act see M. Wood, *The Construction Act: A Practical Guide*. Oxford: Chandos Publishing. . . . . . . . . . . . . . . . . 79

21 The Construction Contracts (England and Wales) Exclusion Order 1998, SI 1998/649; The Construction Contracts (England and Wales) Regulations 1998, SI 1998/648. Both available from the Stationery Office, London . . . . . . . . . . . . . . . . . . . . . . . . . 79

22 Transfer of Undertakings (Protection of Employment) Regulation 1981, SI 1981/1794, reg. 5. Available from the Stationery Office, London . . . . . . . . . . . . . . . . . . . . . . . . . . . . . . . . . . . . . . . . . . . . . . . . 80

23 The Construction (Design and Management) Regulations 1994, SI 1994/3140. Available from the Stationery Office, London. . . . . . . 80

# The Personal Computer in the Small Business

## Efficient Office Practice

**Eamonn Dwyer**

**NCC** Blackwell

MANCHESTER • OXFORD

British Library Cataloguing in Publication Data

Dwyer, E. P.
The personal computer in the small business: efficient office
practice.
1. Great Britain. Small firms. Applications of microcomputer
systems
I. Title
658.0220285416

ISBN 0–85012–797–1

Published for NCC Publications by NCC Blackwell Limited.

Editorial Office, The National Computing Centre Limited, Oxford
Road, Manchester M1 7ED, England.

NCC Blackwell Limited, 108 Cowley Road, Oxford OX4 1JF, England.

Typeset in 10pt Times Roman by Bookworm Typesetting Ltd,
Manchester; and printed by Hobbs the Printers of Southampton.

ISBN 0–85012–797–1

# Foreword

This book is written with users of computers in the small business in mind, and aims, through practical advice, worked examples and exercises, to help those who have taken the initiative to start using a personal computer with little or no training, or who are in the early stages of training. While a person who has displayed such initiative has probably become quite skilful in using a limited range of applications, the facilities offered by the personal computer are not really being exploited. The aim is to lift the level of competence so that the reader begins to take advantage of the potential of the MS-DOS operating system.

In addition, some general issues on information technology are addressed, and the development of microcomputer technology in the context of business use is considered. General information about applications software is also provided, including some practical advice on using a word processor.

The book's aim is to increase readers' levels of skill as quickly and painlessly as possible, so rather than being a comprehensive training scheme, it focuses on a selected set of operating system utilities whose application will enable users to tap much more fully the potential of the personal computer. For that reason, the book has relevance to all computer users with *entry level* skills, including business users, educationalists, medical and caring professionals, students, authors, journalists and researchers.

**Note:** Information in this book is applicable to MS-DOS, Versions 2 and later.

Eamonn Dwyer
October 1989

# Contents

# Introduction
## The Computer as a Resource

Information technology appropriately applied could provide the decisive edge in a very competitive commercial market, yet it is not unusual in the small business to find that the office computer has done little to transform the office work since its arrival, nor has it resulted in any improvement in the trading performance of the business. In effect, the computer as a resource is being under-exploited. This may be because the necessary skills have not yet been acquired by users, or they do not fully use those they already have.

This situation is not uncommon, for example, where the computer is the sole preserve of a member of the clerical or secretarial staff who is a competent typist, but who has had only very basic training in the use of computers. You may be such a person. If so, further training is needed. This does not imply that your existing skills are redundant. Be assured, they are too valuable an asset for that. Instead, it means that they should be enhanced, and that is what this book assists you to do. Even if your ability at the keyboard is limited, the book is aimed to let you take advantage of what you can already do. As your skills develop, so will your confidence in using the computer, and from this will follow a clearer awareness of the computer as a valuable resource, and a greater willingness to exploit its potential.

The need to improve is not confined to business staff. If you are in an occupation such as teaching or training, you are required to draw up plans and prepare presentation material; as a journalist you compile reports; as a student you write assignments; etc. A computer is an asset to you in such situations, so the advice to the user in the small business is, for the most part, equally relevant to you.

## WAYS TO IMPROVE

This book is not a comprehensive training scheme. Except for some advice on using a word processor, and a general description of spreadsheets, databases and accounts programs, it does not instruct you on how to use business applications software. What it does do is show you how to organise your computer-based work in a structured way, and it does this by focusing on fundamental activities which give you a high degree of control over general computer applications. It achieves this by giving you the information you need when at the keyboard.

Surprisingly, levels of competence can be increased dramatically by quite straightforward changes in practice, for example, by organising the computer's files in a more systematic way, by introducing a standardised back-up procedure, and by adopting a policy to secure and protect computer processed data. If such ideas or terms are new to you, do not worry, the book will cover all of these topics in detail. To help you, there are plenty of practical examples to try out, and exercises (with solutions) to let you check your progress in acquiring the necessary skills.

## THE OUTCOME

When you finish this book, you should be able to

- apply a range of newly acquired skills to your computer practice;
- implement a structured approach to the way you organise your work on the computer;
- process information speedily and accurately;
- use the computer with greater efficiency when implementing new applications.

# Plan of the Book

The book has three parts:

**Part I**, Chapters 1 to 4 – This part briefly considers the ways information technology affects our daily lives and places the use of information technology in the small business in this context. It then presents, in general terms, an overview of small business applications of the IBM compatible microcomputer. A final chapter serves as a practical introduction to the MS-DOS operating system by examining approaches to disk organisation.

**Part II**, Chapters 5 to 8 – This part begins by identifying some principles for organising file management on disks. Ways of using word processors to greater effect are also featured, followed by practical advice on developing the MS-DOS command language applications, extending the facilities covered in Part I. Backing-up files receives detailed consideration, and proposals for securing data are discussed.

**Part III,** Chapters 9 to 10 – This part looks at the more advanced topics of creating batch files and configuring the computer system. Although the content of this part is more complex than that in the previous sections, it maintains the practical approach adopted earlier, and capitalises on MS-DOS skills already acquired, so that the unsophisticated user is able to implement the programs provided.

Finally there are appendices on microcomputer systems other than those using MS-DOS, communications, MS-DOS version 4, answers to the end-of-chapter exercises, and a book list for further reading.

# Part I

This part fills in the background to the use of information technology in different contexts, discusses aspects of the development of microcomputer technology, and introduces ways of organising disks.

**Chapter 1: Information Technology**

This chapter provides an introduction to the concept of *information technology*. It starts by considering the meaning and use of the term *information*, and develops the idea by discussing it in relation to *information centres* in the place of work, in the home, and elsewhere. This is further developed into a definition of information technology and its applications in the home and in the world of work.

**Chapter 2: The Microcomputer in the Small Business**

This chapter starts by distinguishing between different types of computer, and clarifies the distinction between *hardware* and *software*. It then goes on to define the term *personal computer* as used in the book, and considers some of the developments in personal computer technology and how this concerns business users.

**Chapter 3: Applications Software**

This chapter is concerned with software which is typically used in the business world. Before looking at specific types, the differences between *programs* and *data* are enunciated, and a distinction is made between *applications* and *system* software. After a brief description of the latter, applications software is categorised as open-ended, application specific, and user specific.

Within these categories, some basic information about word processors is provided, then a more detailed description of spreadsheets and databases is presented, followed by a section about accounts software and its applications. Finally, the implications of commissioning bespoke software are briefly discussed.

**Chapter 4: Disk Organisation**

This chapter starts by defining the term *file*, then goes on to distinguish between *floppy disks* and *hard disks*. An examination is then made of the way disks are organised into four main areas: Boot Record, File Allocation Table, Root Directory and Data Area. This is followed by an introduction to some operating system commands for manipulating disk directories.

# 1 Information Technology

Whether you are a manager of a company with employees, a secretary working in a general office or workshop, or a sole trader, it is not unlikely that you have heard commentators on business affairs talk about the *information explosion* currently transforming the world of commerce and industry. There certainly has been a jargon explosion, making it difficult to know what pundits are talking about. Terms such as information explosion can be slipped into discussion and you nod knowingly, often because you do not wish to show your ignorance. You feel that these terms have something to do with computers, something which you feel you should know about, but haven't had the time or opportunity to find out.

## INFORMATION

Surprisingly, perhaps, your difficulty may lie in the way you perceive information. It is not unusual for people involved in business to feel that 'if only there wasn't so much paperwork' they could really get down to business. What is often not realised is that paperwork is part of the life-blood of the business. It represents a large part of the information which is necessary for the successful operation of the business: customer orders, purchases, stock inventories, accounts, and so on.

Information in this sense is therefore important and any person handling it should do so in a systematic and structured way. This applies as much to letters and reports as to any other information handling. Whether employee or owner, or someone whose business is information such as an instructor, journalist or student, if you are disorganised in dealing with information, your work output is certain to suffer. This is where a computer can help. However, a word of warning, a computer by itself does not create order where chaos reigns. Introducing order is a precondition to efficient and effective computer use, but having done so, the computer can greatly reduce the time and effort required to maintain order, and so provide you with the resource which gives your business or enterprise the competitive edge.

But before looking at how the computer can help in this way, let us first examine how information is central to our lives in all spheres of activity. We do this by considering the notion of *information centres* and how we relate to them in different aspects of our lives. Then it is easier to understand how we might function better in business or in professional roles by harnessing the power of the computer to organise and structure information processing in the work situation.

**Information Centres**

First of all, it would not be unrealistic to describe a business as an information centre. Information pours into it daily in the shape of invoices, payments, advertising literature, newspapers, journals, telephone calls, personal callers' enquiries and transactions, and so on. Information is also relayed from the business to the outside world in much the same manner, although it is likely to be processed in some way beforehand; for example, it may have been created, or modified. Hence, there are three, interdependent but distinct, phases in the information cycle:

- receiving information;

- processing information;

- conveying information.

These take place in addition to, but in association with, the manufacture or assembly of a product, or the provision of a service.

The information handled in a business enterprise must be dealt with in all three phases with great care and precision. The form of this handling is likely to be highly structured and predetermined, that is, it should not be subjected to casual treatment. The content of the information – that is, what message is communicated on the telephone, what amount is set out in the invoice, etc – is determined by business events.

A place of business is not the only information centre we inhabit, although other situations generally place different kinds of demands on us. The home is a prime example. Here we receive a vast amount of information daily, much of it through the same media as in a business, for example, through letters, telephone calls, newspapers and personal callers. In addition, television and radio play a major part. For the most part, however, information in the home is not processed in the same way as in a business. We treat much of it with a high degree of informality. For example, television programmes or newspaper reports are recounted with a generous flavouring of our own views; or a somewhat disastrous attempt to cook a new recipe may be discussed with a good deal of banter, rather than through a detailed analysis of what went wrong.

Although less frequent, certain types of information do, by necessity, receive a more formal approach. Electricity bills, the completion of job application forms, or the scrutiny of a child's school report are cases in point. Correspondence from, say, solicitors or estate agents also falls into this category.

Information conveyed out of the home takes the form of letters, telephone calls, payment of bills and so on, but most is informal output, for example, in the form of chatting with friends or colleagues about television programmes, narration of events which took place or which were reported in the home, descriptions of the new bathroom decor, and so on.

But during the course of a day we are active in other information centres, for example, when we go shopping, ride on public transport, or visit places of entertainment. The form and content of the phases in the different information centres vary according to their social contexts. A visit to a news-stand to buy a paper represents a narrow and limited interaction so the phases have restricted form and minimal content. On the other hand an evening at a disco or restaurant with a group of friends has a form which is characteristically relaxed, and a content which is ordinarily wide ranging and without any particular focus. In such cases the form matters much more than the content.

We therefore exist in many networks of information centres. Moving from one to another generally presents us with little difficulty. We have learned over the years how to behave in each. If we do not conform to the expected approach in handling information according to the social norms of the network, difficulties can arise. For example, if we were to treat a business client too informally, relationships may become strained and a breakdown in the information cycle could ensue with the resulting loss of business. On the other hand, treating our family members as we do business clients causes relationships in the home to suffer.

## INFORMATION TECHNOLOGY

Clearly, then, we have considerable experience in handling information, but let us focus now on the *form*, that is, the means by which information is received, conveyed or processed. Each mode of delivery, whether it reaches us through letters, telephone calls, newspapers, television, word of mouth or by some other means, represents a technology. Technology, in this sense, is nothing new. Human beings at the dawn of civilisation used technology when they created paintings on the walls of cave dwellings. Much later in the history of humankind, the development of written language provided us with a technology which allows us to be very precise in handling information. The printing press, even in its initial stages of development, equipped us with such a powerful technology that its impact on history is inestimable.

What we are concerned with here is technology characteristic of information handling, that is, *information technology*. It is almost as old as the human race itself, yet the term information technology has, in recent years, taken on a more specific meaning. It was first used in the 1970s when the rapid developments in computer technology began to change radically the way information was processed.

Although the application of computers to information processing is central to modern information technology, the term refers to a broad spectrum of electronically based ways of handling information, including telecommunications, broadcasting and consumer electronics, and even includes the use of computers to control machines.

### Information Technology in Everyday Life

In our daily lives, because of these recent changes, the effects of information technology impinge upon us continually. Automatic cash dispensers are an example in which a computer is managing the process. Payment of car tax, or of electricity and similar bills results in computers updating data about us. No-one seems able to escape the intrusion of unsolicited circulars through the mail – we can blame the application of information technology for that because personalising many thousands of letters and addressing envelopes is now a simple task for a computer system.

We may regret the ways information technology has invaded our lives, particularly in applications which intrude upon individual privacy. The Data Protection Act was introduced to ward off the consequences of its least acceptable uses, but one of the most effective guards against the abuse of information technology is to understand how it is used and to take advantage of its benefits.

## Information Technology in the World of Work

While the impact of information technology on everyday life is considerable, it is mainly the consequence of the application of computers in commerce, industry and government. For the most part we are passive participants, unlike, for example, the business enterprise which uses computers extensively in its information processing activities. The information cycle, as described earlier, is almost entirely computerised in many organisations, particularly large corporate institutions. Indeed, many are completely dependent on its successful operation. The structured nature of information in the business setting was also identified, and although computers can handle less structured information (for example, creative writing), they are particularly efficient in processing the former.

To take an example, a company which manufactures domestic appliances, such as washing machines, refrigerators and freezers, will have departments with specific functions, for example, accounts, sales, purchasing, production, storage, transport and wages. Not only is it necessary to maintain and update accurate records for each department, but it is necessary to integrate information across departments in order to view the work of the company as a whole. All of these tasks are suitable for computers because they are extremely good at storing and processing large amounts of information accurately and speedily.

We are ignoring here the use of information technology in the manufacturing process. Obviously the efficiency of computer controlled production methods is central to successful trading in many manufacturing industries. However, computer control technology in this sense is beyond the scope of this book, which is entirely concerned with information processing, or, as it is often described, data processing.

The small business, by its nature, is unlikely to be formally organised into departments as such, but it is an information centre which handles data pertinent to its trading activities, and people within it will have specific responsibilities which will involve data processing. Since computers designed for data processing in the small business are available at an economic cost, there is no reason why a small business should not take advantage of computer technology. Even in the case of a one-person operation, the use of a computer might reduce the data processing workload considerably, and be the factor which determines that the business is profitable in a very competitive market.

# 2 The Microcomputer in the Small Business

Chapter 1 described how information technology affects us in many ways. Its impact is the direct result of the application of the *microprocessor*. The power of microprocessors is apparent when you think that, individually, they are used to control all sorts of domestic appliances, for example the programmes in washing machines, television remote control devices, and the timing and temperature in microwave ovens. Although the microprocessors which do these kinds of jobs are rather low in capacity compared with others used in industrial applications, such as the manufacture of cars, the examples illustrate their function and indicate their power.

But to talk about microprocessors in terms of what they can do today always projects a conservative indication of their potential. No sooner is a new application described in terms of its astounding power than it is out of date. Almost weekly, without any trade-off in increased size, more powerful chips are being designed and produced. Indeed, there has been a steady decrease in the size of microprocessors while their power has increased. Furthermore, prices have dropped simultaneously. This means that domestic appliances are being built with even more powerful and sophisticated chips without increased cost to the consumer. The implication for computers is obvious.

## THE COMPUTER

The developments described have led to the production of smaller yet more powerful computers. The computer harnesses and extends the power of microprocessors by exploiting their capacity. When used in a domestic appliance, the relatively simple microprocessor is required to carry out a given set of tasks which are fixed in its memory. It cannot undertake any other tasks. A computer, on the other hand, can carry out an enormous range of tasks. This flexibility stems partly from the use of one or more relatively sophisticated microprocessors but also, more importantly, from a system organisation ('architecture') – including memory and other peripheral chips – that allows the computer to be programmed by the user. Computer programmability contrasts with the scope of, say, a washing machine where the user can at best do no more than select one of several preprogrammed sequences. The power of a microcomputer, as with any computer, depends largely on the number and degree of sophistication of its various chips.

## TYPES OF COMPUTER

Let us now consider the term *microcomputer*. What is its relationship to a computer? A microcomputer is really no more than a type of computer, in the same sense that a car is a type of vehicle. It is convenient, nevertheless, to think of computers in three categories, and to state that an essential difference is in the power (and size):

- mainframe

- minicomputer

- microcomputer.

A *mainframe* computer is typically used by a large corporate organisation, a government department, or the military. It is very large and expensive, and will often have a whole room dedicated to housing it. It can be used by many people simultaneously from screens and terminals connected to it often over long distances.

One of the main functions of a mainframe computer in a business setting is to centralise the operation of information processing, ensuring that modifications to data are reflected throughout the system and not just at the point of entry. Furthermore, control is exercised over user access, permitting entry to certain types of information to authorised personnel only, and allowing only certain people to enter or change data. This rigid type of control is necessary to guard against corruption of data, whether accidental or deliberate.

A *minicomputer* is a compact and less expensive form of mainframe, but it is similar in many ways, particularly as a multi-user machine. It usually requires at least one room to house it, although some of the smaller models take up less space. They are often used in much the same way as a mainframe, but they are also very popular with institutes of higher education catering for large numbers of students. In the latter situations, not only are there many users, but the users are also carrying out many different tasks, for example, programming in different languages, word processing, and doing graphics work. This type of use calls for a computer which can be extended and is therefore modular in design.

A *microcomputer* is small enough to sit on a desk top, is by far the cheapest of all types, and is the kind of computer this book is written about. It is less powerful than the others, and is used by an individual, although a group of microcomputers can be linked to form a network controlled by one machine and thus be part of a multi-user system. They can also act as terminals to mainframes and minis.

*Memory* is one of the facilities which indicates the power of a computer. There is no need to enter any detailed discussion about the topic but it is necessary for you to know the difference between *main* memory and *backing* or *storage* memory. The former refers to the memory used by the computer as it works. It comprises a series of chips and is an integral part of the computer. When you switch off the computer, all data held in main memory at that moment is lost. Backing memory, although part of the computer hardware, is really a peripheral device. But, unlike main memory, it stores data permanently and therefore is an essential component. By transferring data from main memory to backing memory before switch-off, it is saved, and can be transferred in the opposite direction when the computer is switched on again. Magnetic disks, which are described in Chapter 4, are the main media for backing storage.

These are crude but convenient distinctions. The problem is that progress in computer technology obliges us to avoid making absolute claims about the limitations of the functions of any category of computer, particularly in view of continuing advances in microprocessor technology. However, this book has one type of microcomputer as its focus, namely the personal computer. We are concerned with it as a self-contained machine rather than as a network terminal, although Appendix B does give some information about the use of the personal computer as a means of accessing large systems through the telephone network.

But before proceeding to consider the personal computer in any detail, it is necessary to examine the meaning of two terms which are universally used about computers, namely, *hardware* and *software*. A convenient way to distinguish between hardware and software is to think of a hi-fi system. This consists of hardware, that is the record player, tape deck, speakers, etc. By itself the hardware cannot produce sound; software in the form of tapes, records or compact discs is required for that. Hence the computer and its various parts (keyboard, screen or monitor, disk drives etc) is hardware, while a word processor is an example of software. And just as quality of sound on a hi-fi is determined by the quality of records played on it, so a computer's power can only be fully exploited by good software. Hence, without software, the computer has no valid application as a business tool. In this chapter, the focus is on hardware. Differences between types of software are examined in Chapter 3. Suffice it to say now that without software, a computer is a lifeless machine.

## THE PERSONAL COMPUTER

The term personal computer, as used in this book, refers to a particular type of microcomputer which was first introduced in 1981 by IBM. As its name implies, it is individually, rather than centrally, controlled. The microcomputer, in its very early days, was a machine for the hobbyist or games enthusiast. There was, however, a dramatic change with the introduction of the Apple II microcomputer in 1977; a machine having commercial application. Interestingly, one of the main reasons for the phenomenal success of the Apple II was the accompanying development of good business software, particularly the spreadsheet VisiCalc. But when IBM introduced its more powerful Personal Computer (IBM PC), it quickly became an industry standard and spawned a huge expansion in the software industry. The day of the microcomputer as merely a hobbyist machine had gone for good.

In the wake of the introduction of the IBM Personal Computer, many computer companies have developed clones of the IBM machine (known as IBM compatibles); that is, these machines are assembled using similar architecture, and are able to run almost all of the same software. They are often cheaper and, in many cases, more efficient, and have made computer power available at a cost-effective price to users with very limited budgets.

Among the best known of the British products are the Amstrad PC1512 and the Amstrad PC1614. (The machines are assembled in the UK, but the components are imported – this applies to the manufacture of most microcomputers.) Other clone manufacturers include Opus, Tandon, Viglen (all British), Epson (Japanese), ARC (US), Dell (US – mail order with UK outlet) and Tulip (Dutch).

## Developments in Microcomputer Technology

The pace of development in microcomputer technology has not slackened. IBM has since introduced the more advanced PS/2 models, the more powerful of which offer features which only mainframes or minis could provide a few years ago. Some machines are capable of carrying out more than one task simultaneously (multi-tasking), and they can act as a central facility for more than one user (multi-user). (This latter function, as pointed out earlier, is not new as microcomputers could always act as hosts to a network of less powerful machines, but the latest models do it with much greater efficiency.) And, as happened with the earlier Personal Computer models, clones of the PS/2 are readily available and have forced the price down.

You probably wonder, would a small business want one of these newer models? There are several reasons for answering in the affirmative. First of all, they operate much faster than the earlier models and that may appeal to some. Second, they are better suited to expansion, particularly memory expansion. Third, should a firm consider that it would benefit from having a network of computers at some time in the future, one of these machines would probably be appropriate as a starter. Fourth, there is no doubt that new and exciting software will be developed to exploit the power of the new machines. Fifth, any business thinking of producing its own high quality, printed material, perhaps for publicity literature or reports, should consider this option. Finally, manufacturers tend to stop supporting the older machines. In spite of these reasons for using the newer machines, however, the earlier models have the power and facilities required for many business and non-business applications.

Unlike the earlier personal computers, this new generation is not one basic model. Indeed there are two main types with major differences in the way they are constructed. Each type also offers a variety of options. This means that there are considerable price variations according to the power of processor chips, type of screen, size of memory, and so on. It also means that choice is not quite so straightforward, but this may be beneficial to the prospective purchaser who can obtain exactly what is required initially, but who then has a machine which can be expanded at a later date. The other good news is that they can run the software which was developed for the earlier personal computers, so anyone changing up will not have a major software reinstallation job to contend with.

Quite often, these latest machines are referred to as personal computers, and although this may confuse the newcomer to computing, it is not an important distinction as far as this book is concerned. The practical advice provided in subsequent chapters is applicable to the older and newer varieties of machines. The only requirement is that both types are using the MS-DOS operating system. The meaning of this is clarified in Chapter 4, so there is no need to be concerned with it at present.

We must not entirely overlook the existence of other types of microcomputers which could be used in the small business, such as the Apple Macintosh, the Acorn Archimedes, and the Atari ST. Differences will not be examined here; they are mentioned simply for the sake of completeness, but are discussed briefly in Appendix A. (**Note:** You will come across the term, personal computer, being used to describe these other types of microcomputer. In this sense the term means any desk-top system. However, in this book it has the specific meaning already defined.)

In conclusion, it is apparent that the world of the microcomputer is characterised by rapid change and development. It is an exciting world, but there is a complexity about it which can be threatening to the newcomer. The aim of this book is to reduce this threat by showing you how the application of a selected set of software facilities can give you considerable control over your personal computer, and provide the basis for the development of higher levels of competence.

## EXERCISES

2.1  Explain the difference between hardware and software.

2.2  What distinguishes a personal computer from a mainframe or a minicomputer?

2.3  What is required to make a computer a useful business tool?

2.4  Explain the terms, multi-tasking and multi-user.

2.5  Explain the difference between main memory and storage memory.

# 3 Applications Software

In Chapter 2, you saw that without software the computer has no application as a business tool. It is the software that does the information processing jobs for which microcomputers are renowned, so any book which is concerned with exploiting the computer as a business tool is essentially a book about software. There are different ways to categorise software. The first we look at is the distinction between *program* software and *data* software.

## PROGRAMS AND DATA

A program is a collection of instructions, and data is information upon which the program acts. To explain the difference, let us take an analogy from everyday life. A department store which sells clothing has socks which are selling at £1.50 a pair. You think of buying 3 pairs, and to work out how much money you need, you use a simple formula: 'the number of pairs times the cost of one pair'. The formula is the program, and 1.50 and 3 are data.

Another example is making a cup of coffee, where we go through a routine which can be translated into a set of instructions:

1   fill container 1 with liquid;

2   boil the liquid;

3   put a measure of powder into container 2 etc.

The instructions are the program; and kettle (for container 1), water (for liquid), spoonful (for measure), and cup (for container 2) are data.

## SYSTEM SOFTWARE AND APPLICATIONS SOFTWARE

Programs can be further categorised as *system* software and *applications* software. The latter includes software packages used extensively in the business world, for example, word processors, spreadsheets, databases and accounts software. These packages are described in outline in this chapter and although we return to consider the use of word processors in somewhat more detail in Chapter 5, information about applications software is illustrative rather than instructional. The aim is to sketch in background rather than fill in fine detail, and to set the scene for later chapters where we look at specific ways of using the system software to greater advantage.

### System Software

System software, also known as the *operating system*, is made up of programs which control or manage the operation of the computer system as a whole. It is only through the operating system that applications software can run. It is like a layer which acts as an interface between the computer and applications software (see Figure 3.1).

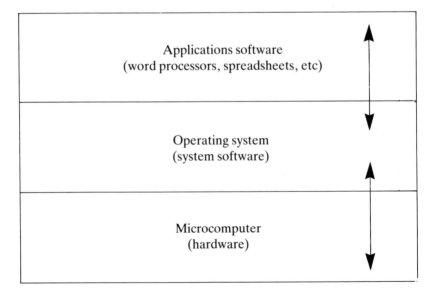

**Figure 3.1   The Operating System in Relation to the Hardware and the Applications Software**

The operating system used on all personal computers is known as MS-DOS, except on IBM personal computers which use PC-DOS. However, for all practical purposes, both systems are the same and are made up of a collection of programs some of which are on the floppy disk you use to start up your computer, or, if you have one, on the hard disk. (DOS stands for disk operating system, and MS for MicroSoft, the creators of MS-DOS.) We return to the operating system in Chapter 5, the first of several chapters which focus on the use of MS-DOS, but we now go on to consider applications software.

### Applications Software

Applications software can be divided into three general categories:

1 *Open-ended software* packages are designed to perform functions with universal business application in information processing contexts and include word processors, spreadsheets and databases. Size of business is irrelevant. They are available off-the-peg from all software dealers, and sell in huge numbers making them relatively inexpensive.

2 *Application-specific software* comprises systems which are dedicated to a specific function. As far as small businesses are concerned they tend to fall under the description of accounts software, for example, payroll or sales ledger.

3 *User-specific software* refers to systems which are commissioned to suit the needs of individual users, for example, an advertiser might want a package which categorises poster sites in relation to location, size, visibility, shape, etc, and be able to measure their value in the context of the advertised product's sales performance. User-specific software, however, is very seldom required in a small business.

The distinctions between these categories are not always clear-cut. Itemised pay statements, for example, which would appear to be a function of payroll software, can be produced by spreadsheets, and the printing of invoices can be accomplished by a word processor. Packages which are designed for general use may, with a small degree of customising, meet the needs of a particular user. Nevertheless, the categories are useful in laying down general guidelines which we use when describing what the software does. Each category is taken in turn, starting with open-ended systems.

**WORD PROCESSORS**

Word processors are bought as ready-to-use packages, and are without doubt the most universal of all applications software; they are perhaps the only computer application whose function requires no more than a cursory explanation to even the most inexperienced computer user. Because we look at them in more detail in Chaper 5, there is no need to devote much space to them here. However, it is worth outlining some of the facilities they offer.

Regardless of product, all word processors have common basic facilities which are a definite asset to anyone who works with words. This is because they give almost complete control over the way you can handle text. They allow you to modify it, store it in permanent form, retrieve it and modify it again, and format it to your liking for printing, and so on. They make it easy for you to delete text, to move text around the document, and to copy text. Nowadays even the more basic packages provide a very wide range of features, for example, a spelling checker and a generous number of fonts. Features are more sophisticated and complex in some packages, but it is best to choose the package which suits your needs rather than one whose main selling point is the range of 'bells and whistles' it offers.

Although they are the most popular of all applications software, they are the least standardised in the sense that, while many of their functions are the same, the commands to execute them vary widely. This means that even with experienced users considerable time may be required to learn new packages.

**SPREADSHEETS**

Computerised spreadsheets, like word processors, are generally bought as ready-to-use packages. They derive from the manual equivalent of a firm's accounts *spread* out on a large *sheet* of paper. Figure 3.2 illustrates this idea. It shows the output from a spreadsheet (or *worksheet*, as it is often called) which has calculated profits over a year for an ice-cream trader. It is laid out as it would be on a sheet of paper; it is logical, intelligible, and easy to use. In other words, the computerised spreadsheet assimilates your way of book-keeping, thus relieving you of the need to adapt to an unfamiliar approach which other types of software might require.

Polar Ices Ltd
Monthly Profit on Sales of Ice-cream
(in £000)

| | A | B | C | D | E | F | G | H | I | J | K | L | M | N | O |
|---|---|---|---|---|---|---|---|---|---|---|---|---|---|---|---|
| | | | Jan | Feb | Mar | Apr | May | Jun | Jul | Aug | Sep | Oct | Nov | Dec | TOTAL |
| 1 | | | | | | | | | | | | | | | |
| 2 | Sales | | 10 | 13 | 11 | 27 | 31 | 29 | 43 | 100 | 91 | 88 | 32 | 76 | 551 |
| 3 | | | | | | | | | | | | | | | |
| 4 | Expenditure | 17 | 15 | 15 | 19 | 20 | 19 | 22 | 41 | 29 | 20 | 20 | 30 | | 267 |
| 5 | | | | | | | | | | | | | | | |
| 6 | Profit | | −7 | −2 | −4 | 8 | 11 | 10 | 21 | 59 | 62 | 68 | 12 | 46 | 284 |
| 7 | | | | | | | | | | | | | | | |
| 8 | | | | | | | | | | | | | | | |
| 9 | | | | | | | | | | | | | | | |

**Figure 3.2   Spreadsheet Output Showing Columns and Rows**

**Spreadsheet Size and Screen Size**

The output from spreadsheets may be very large. Their application would be severely restricted if it were limited to the size of the screen. What you see on the screen is a window to one small section of the full worksheet. To see a particular section of the spreadsheet not visible on the screen, you move it into the window with the cursor keys (see Figure 3.3).

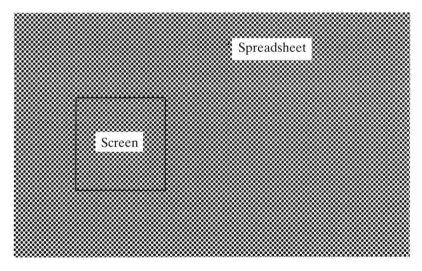

**Figure 3.3   The Screen as a Window to a Spreadsheet**

**Columns and Rows**

Flexibility is one of the major features characterising a spreadsheet, and yet it is based on the simple model of a financial worksheet made up of an array of columns and rows. The intersections of the columns and rows are known as cells (their locations identified by column letter and row number), and it is the cells which are the main elements of the spreadsheet. They receive, store and display different types of data, namely:

- text

- numbers

- formulae.

The text is used as labels to identify the numerical values in the spreadsheet; the numbers are the raw data on which the spreadsheet works; and the formulae hold the instructions for manipulating the numbers.

Figure 3.2 illustrates the use of all three data types. Most of the data on display is self-explanatory, but the numbers in the cells along row 6, are the results of calculations carried out by formulae entered in each. For example the formula in C6 is C2-C4, and the formula in O2 is C2+D2+E2..etc.

**Benefits of Using a Spreadsheet**

Why use a spreadsheet if it merely represents a computerised version of a manual system which can do a good job and costs much less to set up? To answer this, refer to Figure 3.2 again, and think what would have to be done in a manual system if you discovered that two input errors had been made; for example, that the Sales for May (cell G2) should be 29, and the Expenditure for October (cell L4), 35. A complete recalculation would be necessary for the Profits in May (G6) and October (L6), for the Total Sales (O2) and Expenditure (O4), and for the Total Profits (O6). A spreadsheet instantly updates all cells affected by the entry of revised amounts. Hence speed of calculation and accuracy are assured (providing, of course, that the input is correct). The savings in your time could easily offset the expense incurred in setting up the computerised system.

The only limits to the use of a spreadsheet for a book-keeping system are those imposed by limits of imagination. It can be used, for example, to set up ledgers, balance sheets, and profit and loss statements. It can also be used as a database. But its flexible and creative potential lies in its ability to provide a model in which possible or proposed changes in financial circumstances can be tested. Often referred to as *what-if?* analysis, you could, for example, test the effects of changes in expenditure.

### What-Ifing with Spreadsheets

Figure 3.4 is an expanded version of Figure 3.2, showing a breakdown of Expenditure into Wages, Raw Materials, Transport, Advertising, and Miscellaneous. The finer detail enables possible or proposed changes in expenditure to be more accurately assessed; for example, if it were discovered that milk could be obtained more cheaply from another supplier, the amounts in Row 6 could be modified and the effect on profits examined. However, the different milk might result in a change in the taste of the ice-cream, making increased expenditure on advertising necessary. The effect of this could likewise be tested on the spreadsheet.

Polar Ices Ltd
Monthly Profit on Sales of Ice-cream
(in £000)

| | A | B | C | D | E | F | G | H | I | J | K | L | M | N | O |
|---|---|---|---|---|---|---|---|---|---|---|---|---|---|---|---|
| 1 | | | Jan | Feb | Mar | Apr | May | Jun | Jul | Aug | Sep | Oct | Nov | Dec | TOTAL |
| 2 | Sales | | 10 | 13 | 11 | 27 | 31 | 29 | 43 | 100 | 91 | 88 | 32 | 76 | 551 |
| 3 | | | | | | | | | | | | | | | |
| 4 | Expenditure | | | | | | | | | | | | | | |
| 5 | Wages | | 8 | 7 | 7 | 8 | 9 | 9 | 10 | 24 | 12 | 9 | 9 | 12 | 124 |
| 6 | Raw Mat | | 5 | 4 | 4 | 5 | 5 | 6 | 5 | 8 | 8 | 5 | 5 | 8 | 68 |
| 7 | Transport | 2 | 1 | 1 | 2 | 2 | 2 | 2 | 4 | 4 | 2 | 2 | 4 | | 28 |
| 8 | Advertising | 1 | 1 | 1 | 2 | 2 | 2 | 2 | 4 | 4 | 3 | 3 | 5 | | 30 |
| 9 | Misc | | 1 | 2 | 2 | 2 | 2 | 2 | 1 | 1 | 1 | 1 | 1 | 1 | 17 |
| 10 | Total Exp | | 17 | 15 | 15 | 19 | 20 | 19 | 22 | 41 | 29 | 20 | 20 | 30 | 267 |
| 11 | | | | | | | | | | | | | | | |
| 12 | Profit | | −17 | −12 | −14 | 8 | 11 | 10 | 21 | 59 | 62 | 68 | 12 | 46 | 284 |
| 13 | | | | | | | | | | | | | | | |
| 14 | | | | | | | | | | | | | | | |
| 15 | | | | | | | | | | | | | | | |

**Figure 3.4    A Spreadsheet Showing a Breakdown of Expenditure**

The spreadsheet is capable of carrying out tasks of much greater complexity than those described here. Yet the principle of its operation is not complex. Rather, complexity is an indication of the spreadsheet's power in applying such a simple principle. Certainly, the most recent versions are offering radical improvements by introducing systems with three-dimensional tables. But although these are undoubtedly instruments of considerable power, they nevertheless do not depart from the underlying concept of columns, rows and cells. (**Note:** Some of the recent, more powerful databases may require computers with a large amount of main memory, perhaps more than 640K.)

## DATABASES

Databases, unlike word processors and spreadsheets, often need a fair amount of preparation before they can be run, and customising is necessary in many cases. This may require the services of a programmer, although a member of staff who has undergone some training for the particular package might manage it. They are used for storing information which needs to be referred to regularly and for writing reports, and they deal with information as it exists, unlike spreadsheets which let you test the effects of possible changes. But databases, which can handle huge amounts of data, let you extract pieces of information according to specific conditions rather than merely regurgitate the data as you entered it.

### Structure of a Database

A simple example is a Member Database for a compact disc mail-order club. You can think of it as a sort of card index system or file which contains *records*, each record holding the same type of information about an individual member: for example, name; address; telephone number; most recent order; discs received; discs paid for; and debts outstanding. These groupings of information are held in *fields*, so you have a database which consists of three levels: a file which contains records, which, in turn, contains fields. This type of system is often referred to as a *flat file database* (see figure 3.5).

Like a spreadsheet, the data is stored in a structured way. Indeed, there are many similarities between the two systems. They are both two-dimensional, with the rows in the spreadsheet being equivalent to records, and the columns to fields. The organisation of fields in records means that they are more manageable. It is easy to find information such as names of members who live in the same town, or draw up a list of those who have bought more than two compact discs during the previous month.

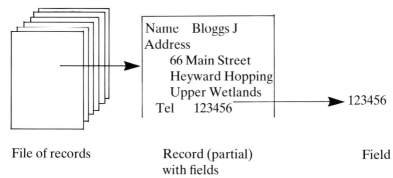

File of records                    Record (partial)                        Field
                                      with fields
**Figure 3.5    The Relationship between a File, a Record and a Field in a Database**

### Replicating Information on Records

The information contained in the Member Database would typically be used for recurring tasks, such as printing mailing labels to send monthly catalogues, updating accounts, notifying payment defaulters, and identifying members who have placed orders but whose accounts are outstanding. Information of this type is easy to store, update and retrieve.

Yet there must be a trade-off between amount of information stored and time to process it. For example, if the information on the most recent order also includes compact disc number, manufacturer's name and address, supplier's name and address, disc title, musical category, performer's name, price, etc, each record becomes inordinately large. Large amounts of data are replicated because many customers ordering the same disc results in identical information about that disc being held on several customers' records. The result is slower access time because the computer is forced to read the same data over and over.

### Relational Databases

One way to overcome this difficulty is to use a *relational database*. In essence, a relational database is a collection of flat file databases linked together. For example, by using two flat file databases in place of the single file Member Database you could keep details about members in one, the Member Database, and details about discs in the other, the Disc Database. To link them, you have one field common to both, in this case, disc number. This common field forges the relationship between the databases, hence the term relational database. To take an example, if Mary Ford, Jim Morris and Rachel Austin all order disc 1452, then their records in the Member Database can be linked to the appropriate record in the Disc Database through the disc number, thereby avoiding the duplication of data in the former (see Figure 3.6). If 50 members order the same disc, there is an obvious saving in both main memory and storage disc space, and access time is speeded up accordingly.

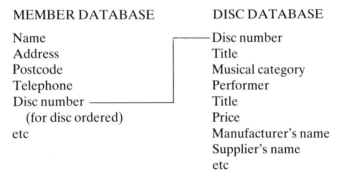

**Figure 3.6    Linking Records via Disc Number**

You can carry this refinement further by creating a Manufacturer Database and a Supplier Database, perhaps linking the Disc Database to both, as illustrated in Figure 3.7. Relational databases are generally much more complex than this, but the system illustrated does convey the basic concept.

While using the example of a collection of linked flat file databases is an effective way of explaining how a relational database works, it is a more complicated system to implement and use. So, unless you are able to justify its application in terms of improved business efficiency, you should question the need for it. To use a relational database when, for example, a flat file database is just as able to do your job is definitely an example of taking a very large sledgehammer to crack a very small nut.

To learn to use a relational database is a time-consuming task, and, to start with, considerable preparation is needed to set it up. Indeed,

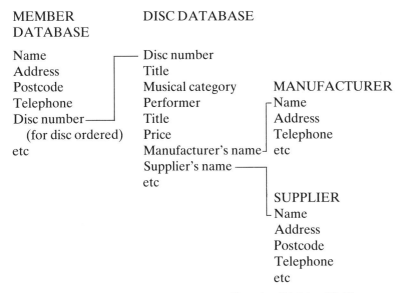

**Figure 3.7   A Relational Database Showing Linking Fields**

installing a relational database on your personal computer is a programming exercise (relational databases have their own programming languages), and while it is not essential to secure the services of a programmer to implement a system, it might be advisable to do so unless someone in your business has had considerable experience in the use of the package. Alternatively, a member of staff who is competent in using a single file database, and thoroughly understands the way it works, could probably develop the skills necessary to set up a relational database, but it would not be achieved overnight. In fact, you would have to see this course of action as a long-term solution. But if your business would benefit from the use of a relational database, then you should not let the difficulties prevent its installation and implementation.

## INTEGRATED SOFTWARE

There are many packages which integrate spreadsheets and databases; indeed most include word processors as well. Their major feature is that data entered in, say, the database, becomes available to the spreadsheet, and in the best packages updating occurs automatically throughout the system. A drawback is that the elements in the system are not generally as powerful in application as individual spreadsheet, database or word processing packages. However, many small businesses do not need such power, so an integrated package is more appropriate, particularly the spreadsheet and database. Word processors are perhaps a different matter as their advanced features can be used to advantage, regardless of size and scope of business. This issue will be taken up in Chapter 4, but if you have an integrated package, or are considering purchase, then you should see if the word processor might be a useful asset, particularly for some jobs related to the spreadsheet and database.

## APPLICATION-SPECIFIC SOFTWARE

The second category of applications software is application-specific software. It is designed to carry out specific tasks. Among the best known example is software which takes care of different aspects of accounting, for example, payroll and nominal ledger. However, it does not in itself organise your accounting activities; it is a tool to be applied to existing, well organised manual systems. But a successful computerised system brings considerable benefits. It is possible, for example, to produce a Profit and Loss Account showing the current financial state of your business without having to wait for an accountant to collect all the information at a particular time of the year. In fact, you could produce a report as often as you wish. This does not imply that the services of an accountant may be dispensed with; it means, instead, that you are not as dependent on these services, and that you are in a position to closely monitor business performance continually.

The most common applications for which accounts packages have been written are:

Stock Control                       – deals with additions to, removals from, and the storing of trading stock.

Purchase Ledger                     – deals with the purchasing of stock.

Invoicing and Sales Ledger          – deals with the sales of goods, either manufactured or from stock, or services.

Payroll                             – facilitates the calculation of wages.

Nominal Ledgers                     – bring together the various totals from the other ledgers under classified headings for financial analysis up to, and sometimes including, the final accounts.

Accounting systems may be fully integrated, that is, all of the systems together can be regarded as a single system with the different functions (Purchase Ledger, etc) as subsystems. But many businesses use individual systems with manual inter-system transactions. Another approach is to use a package which is more akin to a cash book accounting system. These are suited to businesses which operate a 'cash-in cash-out' book-keeping system. Of course, a spreadsheet may be an appropriate tool in these circumstances, particularly as it should allow the implementation of a system similar to the manual one already in use.

## USER-SPECIFIC SOFTWARE

Some businesses feel that off-the-peg packages do not cater for their needs, and so decide to commission user-specific software (known as *bespoke* software). It is a highly expensive undertaking as a great amount of time is spent in its preparation. One of the major problems which arises from the use of this type of software, is that it can be very inflexible, and if the information processing system in the business undergoes any restructuring, the software may need major rewriting to accommodate the changes. Also, those who commission it often discover that they have not been precise enough in defining their needs, or that the programmer has misinterpreted their requirements; the result is that they are left with a system which does not do what they want.

So if you think that your business would benefit from bespoke software, seek the services of a reputable consultant, that is a person who can analyse the information system in your enterprise, and who will ensure that the software you receive is properly installed and supported. It is also likely that training in the use of the software will be required; make sure not only that this is part of the deal, but also that it is effective.

Very often the answer lies in having existing software customised. Furthermore, bespoke software, after installation, may be sold to other users as off-the-peg products, so you should look around to see if there is anything on offer. But even then it is expensive as the market for it is likely to be very small. Whichever route is taken, be prepared to dig deep in your pocket, but only after you have decided conclusively that no off-the-peg package meets your needs.

**EXERCISES**

3.1 If your car's fuel consumption is 10 kilometres to a litre of petrol and you are about to undertake a 1,000 kilometre journey, what is the program to calculate the total fuel required, and what is the data required for the calculation?

3.2 Explain the difference between a flat file database and a relational database.

3.3 If you were a car dealer who sells and services ten different models, and you decide to set up a relational database to help you keep track of customers, and cars sold to and serviced for them, what files would you construct, and what information would you store in each?

3.4 What is the similarity in structure between a flat file database and a spreadsheet?

# 4 Disk Organisation

## INTRODUCTION

*File* is one of those ubiquitous terms in computing, the meaning of which many writers regard as being self-evident. However, it very often confuses newcomers to computing so a definition at this stage should help. It is also appropriate to clarify its meaning now because the purpose of disk organisation is to create a systematic approach to file storage on disks.

To put it simply, a file is a collection of data which is stored on a disk (or any storage medium), and which has a *filename*. A program similarly stored is also a file. If you write a letter to Smith Ltd using a word processor, then you save it on a disk under a filename, say SMITH, you have created a file containing data, that is a *data file*. By the same token a file which contains a program is a *program file*.

### Conventions Used in the Book for Keyboard Instructions

**Note:** When instructions for actually using your computer are given in this book, certain conventions have been adopted:

1 To let you know that you are to enter commands or filenames from the keyboard, the term *key-in* is used.

2 When you see the symbols < and > around a word or group of characters, this indicates a key to be pressed, and not a word or characters to be entered. The first example of this you meet is <Return> for the 'Return' or 'Enter' key, which might be indicated on your keyboard by the broken-arrow symbol ⌐. Other examples are <Ctrl> for the 'control key', <Shift> for the 'shift key', <F1> for the 'F1 function key', and <Esc> for the 'escape key'.

## PERMANENT MEMORY

In Chapter 2, you were introduced to the concept of computer memory. It was pointed out that there are two sorts of memory: main memory and backing memory, the latter referring to permanent storage. The main device for storing information permanently on the personal computer is a disk. We are concerned with the two main types, the floppy disk and the hard disk. The computer stores data on disks in the same way technically as sound is stored on a record or audio tape, or sound and visual material on a video tape. There are differences between floppy and hard disks in their design, construction and operation, but they are also very similar in many ways. Each one is considered in turn.

## FLOPPY DISKS

There are two sizes of floppy disk in common use on the personal computer, 5.25 inch and 3.5 inch. The former looks and feels floppy while the latter conceals its floppiness by being enclosed in a rigid plastic case. Both are circular pieces of plastic which spin when in use, very like records on a turntable. And, like the records, a head comes in contact with them, to both *write* (record) data on to their surfaces as well as *read* (play) it. One difference from records is that disks are divided into tracks (like circular roads) and sectors (like slices in a pie) as in Figure 4.1. Also records play concentrically in a continuous manner, whereas data disks can be read or written to just about anywhere; tracks and sectors being used to specify locations to which the head goes directly (the section below on formatting explains this in more detail).

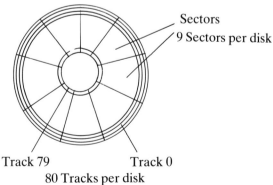

Sectors
9 Sectors per disk

Track 79          Track 0
80 Tracks per disk

**Figure 4.1     Tracks and Sectors on a Floppy Disk**

## HARD DISKS

A hard disk is really a set of rigid disks (platters) set one above the other and rotating about a vertical spindle. The term hard disk refers to the complete set of platters. Each platter is divided into tracks and sectors in much the same way as a floppy disk, and data is stored on and retrieved from it according to the same principles, so in terms of general disk organisation there is little difference between the two types of disk.

However, a hard disk can hold a very large amount of data, at least 50 times as much as a floppy disk, and usually more, and this capacity is continually being increased. Furthermore, because the disk spins at more than ten times the speed of a floppy, transfer of data between disk and computer memory takes place at a much higher speed. One other major difference between a hard and a floppy disk is that the former is fixed in position. It is, in effect, a part of the computer system hardware. This means it is unnecessary to load and unload disks, and programs, including the system programs which start up the computer, are immediately available. (**Note:** A personal computer with a hard disk always has at least one floppy disk drive. This is necessary in order to be able to transfer system software and application software on to the hard disk, and to copy from the hard disk on to a floppy.)

### Advantages and Disadvantages of Hard Disks

To summarise, the advantages of having a hard disk are (i) large storage space, (ii) speed of access to software packages and to data, and (iii) convenience of not having to continually load and unload disks.

The disadvantages are that there is a trade-off in security of data because (i) the fixed location of the hard disk increases the chances of losing data through damage or theft, and (ii) it is more difficult to shield sensitive data from prying, unauthorised eyes. To obviate these risks, it is essential to make regular floppy disk copies of data on a hard disk, that is to back-up data, and also to restrict access to sensitive data by ensuring that the computer is only available to authorised users. These issues are considered further in Chapters 7 and 8.

### ORGANISATION OF STORAGE ON A DISK

Before a disk can be used for the first time, it must be *formatted*. It is also possible to format a disk with data on it, and sometimes this is necessary, but formatting removes all data from the disk (this is not absolutely true, but for all practical purposes we will assume it to be so) so be cautious about which disks you format. In Chapter 6 you are told how to format a floppy disk, but here we look at what happens to a disk when it is formatted. This information helps you to understand how file management on disks is organised.

## FORMATTING DISKS

What does formatting do to a disk? It is a process which divides the disk surface into sections. To understand why these sections are necessary, think of a notebook, where the pages of the book start off as one long strip of paper before it is cut up, collated and bound. We could certainly write on the paper in its continuous form, yet imagine the inconvenience when we wish to find something after a large amount of information has been written on it. By having it in notebook form, this difficulty is avoided; for example, by using the page numbers as guides to finding a particular piece of writing. Even better, if we create chapters and sections, and include a list of contents, we can find the information much more quickly. A disk likewise is divided into sections, during formatting, to facilitate the creation of a kind of indexing system which keeps track of data locations. The computer can then find the data by 'looking up' the index.

### Tracks and Sectors

Instead of pages and chapters, the disk is divided into tracks and sectors (as in Figure 4.1). The tracks are concentric, with double-sided disks having twice as many tracks as single-sided. The tracks are divided into sectors so that the disk is also divided radially. Hence, if a disk consists of 80 tracks, each track being made up of 9 sectors, each of which can hold 512 *bytes* of data (generally speaking, a byte is the equivalent of one keyboard character), then the total capacity of the disk is (80 × 9 × 512) bytes, that is 368,640 bytes, or 360 kilobytes (a kilobyte, or K, is 1,024 bytes). 360K is the typical size of a 5.25 inch, single density floppy disk.

Memory is measured in bytes, so when we say that a disk size is 360K, we mean its memory is 360K. The same system of measurement is used for main memory.

A byte, as explained, is the space required on a disk for one character, a character being any of the symbols, including punctuation marks and spaces, which display on the screen when a key on the keyboard is pressed. In concrete terms, a 360K disk is able to hold a document equal to the length of this book. Although you might think that it would take a long time to fill a disk when writing letters and other short documents, you are underestimating the amount of written information which is produced, even in a small business, each day.

However, it is worth pointing out that the capacity of disks is constantly increasing. For example 1.44 megabytes (M) is now fairly common on 3.5 inch floppy disks, and 1.2M on 5.25 inch disks (a megabyte being 1,024 kilobytes). Hard disks are generally at least 20M, but they also are being supplied in much larger sizes.

**Note:** MS-DOS Versions 2 to 3.3 use a maximum of 32M hard disk space, but this should cause you no concern. If you do own a larger hard disk, it must be partitioned so that each partition is no greater than 32M. This has the effect of making it into two or more *virtual* hard disks which you address as drive C, drive D, etc; thus you treat it as if it were two or more separate pieces of hardware. Instructions on partitioning a hard disk will be found in your computer manual, or, if your hard disk was installed subsequent to purchase of the computer, instructions are in the hard disk manual. (MS-DOS Version 4 can use in excess of 32M; further information is given Appendix C.)

Formatting, however, not only divides the disk as already described. When the tracks and sectors are laid down, it shares the total space among four main areas: (i) the *Boot Record*, (ii) the *File Allocation Table (FAT)*, (iii) the *Root Directory*, and (iv) the *Data Area*.

**Boot Record**

The Boot Record is the software interface between the hardware and the operating system, its function being to call the operating system into action. This is known as *bootstrapping* or *booting-up* (from the expression 'to pull yourself up by your own bootstraps') when the Boot Record actually is instrumental in getting the computer up and going. The operating system, once activated, takes control of the system.

**File Allocation Table**

The File Allocation Table, as the term implies, holds information about files, that is, their length, and where they are to be found on the disk. To relate what happens in the FAT to an everyday situation, we return to the example of the notebook. Imagine you are writing a report on a market research project. You start by entering the title of the report in the list of contents, say:

| | page |
|---|---|
| Market research – new fabric | 6 |

The report takes up four pages. Then another report is written, say, 'Advertising report – TV'. Once again the title and starting page number are entered in the contents:

| | page |
|---|---|
| Advertising report – TV | 10 |

This report takes three pages, so it finishes on page 12. More information comes in from the market research project, and as your notebook is not of the loose-leaf variety, you go to page 13 and continue for five pages. Your report is now broken up, so you need to show in the contents list not only that the report is fragmented, but also where the last entry occurs. One way to accomplish this is to add information to the first entry in the contents list, for example, 'continued page 13', indicating fragmentation, and in the second entry, include 'last part'. (The entry for the advertising report is also shown with 'last part' added.)

| | | page |
|---|---|---|
| Market research – new fabric | (continued page 13) | 6 |
| Advertising report – TV | (last part) | 10 |
| Market research – new fabric | (last part) | 13 |

Should you continue the report at a later time, say on page 40 for two pages (with a report on 'Sales' in between), then 'last part of report' is entered in the contents list, and the previous entry is changed to 'continued on page 40':

| | | page |
|---|---|---|
| Market research – new fabric | (continued page 13) | 6 |
| Advertising report – TV | (last part) | 10 |
| Market research – new fabric | (continued page 40) | 13 |
| Sales – 1988/89 | (last part) | 18 |
| Market research – new fabric | (last part) | 40 |

In essence the same system is used by the FAT to keep track of files on a disk where sectors are the equivalent of pages.

**Root Directory**

The third area which is set aside during formatting of a disk is the Root Directory, or main directory; a directory being conceptually similar to a filing cabinet. The Root Directory is a fixed area of disk space which contains either files or other directories, known as *subdirectories*. To take the analogy further, a subdirectory can be likened to a drawer in a filing cabinet. The directory system is hierarchical, that is, the higher levels encapsulate the lower levels which they contain. The section below, on subdirectories, examines this idea in more detail.

**Note:** Filenames are written in upper-case throughout the book for ease of identification. You are advised to follow this convention, although it is not essential as MS-DOS converts lower-case filenames into upper-case.

The Root Directory is limited in the number of files (and subdirectories) which can be put into it; no more than 112 on a 360K floppy disk, and 512 on a hard disk. However, there is no limit to the number of files or other subdirectories, subject to disk space, that you can put into subdirectories. In other words, while a Root Directory is static in the amount of disk space allocated to it, subdirectories can be created, deleted, expanded and contracted as required.

**Data Area**

This is the last of the four areas created when the disk is formatted. As its name implies it is the area in which all subdirectories and files are actually held other than those used in the Boot Record, the FAT and the Root Directory.

**THE MS-DOS OPERATING SYSTEM**

MS-DOS has a reputation for being difficult to learn, and while there are aspects which can be confusing, even for the experienced user, it includes a set of very useful functions which are easy for the newcomer to grasp. Although relatively small in number, these functions are nevertheless wide-ranging in scope of operation and effect. Some of the operating system jobs, which will be of interest to you, are concerned with file management; for example, formatting floppy disks, changing between directories, creating directories, copying files between disks, and deleting files. These, and many other very useful utilities, are covered in this and later chapters, but first it is necessary to establish that you know how to get to the correct place in the system to enable you to issue MS-DOS commands.

## MS-DOS Command Line

In order to enter MS-DOS commands, it is necessary to be at the *MS-DOS Command Line level* (or, more simply, MS-DOS level). It is probably easier to explain when you are not at MS-DOS level than to explain when you are. When you are using a word processor, a database, or any applications software package, you are not at MS-DOS level, you are at *applications level*. Otherwise, it is likely you are at MS-DOS level. You know for sure when you see one of the three prompts which indicate your current disk drive:

**A>**   or   **B>**   or   **C>**

A and B are floppy disk drives, and C is a hard disk drive. There may be additional information in the prompt, but the drive letter is always present. And when you see expressions in this book such as *enter MS-DOS* and *go into MS-DOS*, they refer to the procedures involved in getting to the level where you can issue MS-DOS commands. It is likely that you will find yourself at MS-DOS level after booting-up your computer.

You may, however, find that the computer you are using is set up so that it does not at any time enter the Root Directory or a subdirectory. For example, after booting-up, a menu might appear on screen which asks you to select from among a number of options for applications programs only (and, of course, an option to close down the computer). Menu interfaces are very convenient, but some, rather surprisingly, do not give you direct access to MS-DOS. If you are in this position, you will have to ask the person who set up the menu to rectify this omission.

## DIRECTORIES AND SUBDIRECTORIES

The MS-DOS system provides the facility to divide a disk into directories and subdirectories. To help you understand what they are, you should first carry out this activity. First, boot-up your computer and wait for the MS-DOS prompt to appear on screen. We now try two commands: (i) to take you into the Root Directory, and (ii) to see what is in the Root Directory. All examples of commands are shown in upper-case, but use lower-case if you wish (MS-DOS converts to upper-case anyway):

(i)  To get to the Root Directory, key-in:

**CD\\<Return>**

CD stands for 'change directory'. The backslash indicates Root Directory when it comes immediately after a command. If you are in the Root Directory to start with, entering CD\ will do no harm. From now on, because pressing <Return> is always used to activate MS-DOS commands after you key them in, this instruction will be omitted.

(ii)  To see what is in the Root Directory, key-in:

**DIR**

and a listing of the contents of your Root Directory appears on screen (DIR stands for 'directory'). Do not try to decipher the listing at present. We will come back to that shortly, but for the present you can reflect that you used two of the most common and useful MS-DOS commands. You have also seen what a directory is, and what sort of things it contains. MS-DOS lets us set up our own directories, and, although the Root Directory is special, all directories have the same form.

## Organisational Structure

The idea of directories and subdirectories grew out of the recognition that data on a hard disk requires an organisational structure which differs radically from that which is perfectly adequate for floppy disks. It takes little imagination to think of what would happen if thousands of files were stored in a single directory on a hard disk; it is akin to storing all your documents in one filing cabinet without any folders or subdivisions.

The computer is, of course, capable of coping with the numerous files in a single directory, but you would have problems in remembering which files are which, or knowing if the files you are looking for are there at all. You are, of course, perfectly entitled to store all your files in the Root Directory, but it will lead to confusion. And do not forget that you are limited to 512 entries in these circumstances. Even if you deal with a relatively small number of files in total, you should use directories and subdirectories because of the benefits you get from the degree of structure and organisation they build into your system.

To give you some idea about the purpose of directories and subdirectories, take a list of cities throughout the world. We could simply view this as a two-level structure as shown in Figure 4.2, which is similar in organisation to a disk with a Root Directory.

This two-level structure presents the same sorts of problems as a disk which has a Root Directory only. Finding particular cities on a map from this information would be a cumbersome task. The search is simplified if we group the cities according to continent as shown in Figure 4.3, where continents represent a lower directory or subdirectory level, and as you can see the organisation makes searching for a city a more straightforward task. There is no need to read through all the city names if we know which continent to look at.

In this analogy, introducing a further level, specifying countries would be even more helpful in a search, as Figure 4.4 shows. However, do not allow yourself to create too many directory levels on a hard disk. Too much depth can make them as unmanageable as having a Root Directory only.

### Self-check Activity

Suggest an additional level which would make cities easier to find on the map of a country.

### Solution

Regions would help, although it might be difficult to think of a system which would be common to all countries.

### Root Directory Entries

Before going on to examine ways in which subdirectories can be organised, it is necessary to point out that certain MS-DOS files must be in the Root Directory because the computer looks for them there when booting-up and if they are missing, it can go no further. It is actually a moot point which files are essential but rather than introduce an issue which may lead to confusion, no distinction is made in this book

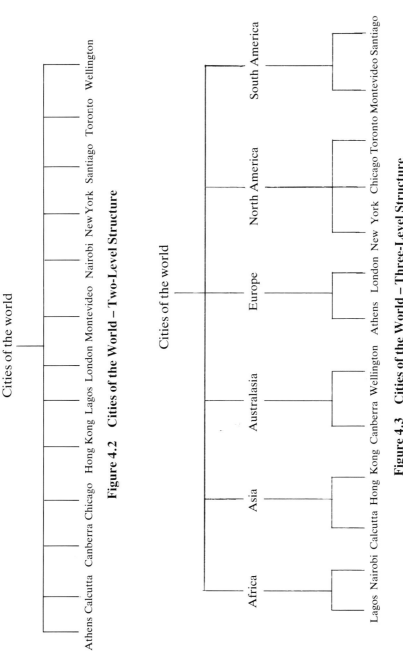

Cities of the world

Athens Calcutta Canberra Chicago Hong Kong Lagos London Montevideo Nairobi New York Santiago Toronto Wellington

**Figure 4.2   Cities of the World – Two-Level Structure**

Cities of the world

Africa   Asia   Australasia   Europe   North America   South America

Lagos Nairobi Calcutta Hong Kong Canberra Wellington Athens London New York Chicago Toronto Montevideo Santiago

**Figure 4.3   Cities of the World – Three-Level Structure**

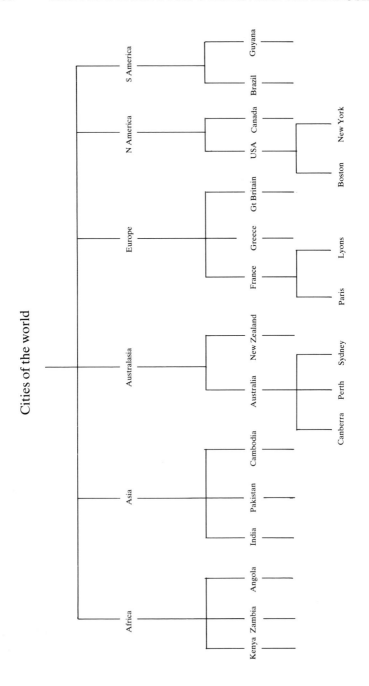

**Figure 4.4   Cities of the World – Four-Level Structure**

between those which are essential and those which are recommended, and together they are regarded as 'required'. To start with, the three files, COMMAND.COM, AUTOEXEC.BAT and CONFIG.SYS are required, together with two hidden files, IOSYS.COM and MSDOS-.COM (these hidden filenames vary in different personal computers, for example, they are named as IO.SYS and MSDOS.SYS in the Amstrad PC1512 and PC1640). If you do not have a hard disk, these five files are required on your boot-up disk.

**Note:** The hidden files do not appear in a directory listing. In Chapter 6, instructions on how to copy them to the boot-up disk are given in the section on the FORMAT command.

Have a closer look now at the files which are in your Root Directory. Do not be surprised, however, if you see a much larger number of entries than those indicated above. Indeed the number may be so large that the listing scrolls off the screen. If so, key-in:

**DIR/P**

instead of DIR (the /P option implying 'one page at a time') and the scrolling stops after each screen page. Alternatively, key-in:

**DIR/W**

and the listing is displayed in five columns instead of the usual one.

A typical Root Directory listing, with a relatively small number of entries, is shown in Figure 4.5. Dates, volume name, and the subdirectory names (the entries followed by <DIR>) will be entirely different on your screen, but your listing will have the same form.

**The Structure of Directories**

As you can gather from what has been said about directories and subdirectories, the difference between them is one of organisation, so the term subdirectory will not be used from now on (unless it is necessary to clarify meaning). In addition, when you examine a listing of files in a subdirectory on screen, you will see 'Directory' at the top, so to avoid confusion this term is preferred.

Figure 4.6 shows an example of part of the WORDS directory which was displayed in the listing in Figure 4.5. The first two lines with the full stops appear at the top of all directories (except in the Root Directory) so we can ignore them. The other entries are program files for the word

Volume in Drive C IS E DWYER HD20
Directory of C:\

| | | | | |
|---|---|---|---|---|
| COMMAND | COM | 23612 | 24–08–87 | 0:00 |
| CONFIG | SYS | 64 | 26–03–87 | 11:02 |
| ANSI | SYS | 1651 | 26–03–87 | 15:21 |
| WORDS | <DIR> | | 28–03–87 | 11:02 |
| BATCH | <DIR> | | 3–06–87 | 22:15 |
| DOS | <DIR> | | 5–10–88 | 10:00 |
| AUTOEXEC | BAT | 185 | 26–03–87 | 10:31 |
| NORTON | <DIR> | | 1–09–89 | 9:11 |
| DATABASE | <DIR> | | 28–03–87 | 11:15 |
| SPRDSHT | <DIR> | | 15–04–87 | 9:57 |
| ABILITY | <DIR> | | 3–02–88 | 15:15 |
| XTPRO | <DIR> | | 1–09–89 | 9:41 |

8 File(s)                        15094528 bytes free

**Figure 4.5    A Listing of Files and Subdirectories in the Root Directory**

processor, WordStar, and data files for this book created by WordStar, the latter having the extension .TXT.

**Creating Directories**

As was pointed out earlier, directories were devised to allow a logical approach to file storage on hard disks. It is possible to create directories on a floppy disk, although they tend not to be used. In fact, it is convenient to think of a floppy as equivalent to a directory. Nevertheless, directories on floppy disks can be very useful, so you can use either floppies or a hard disk for the following activities, the first of which is to create a directory called WORDS.

The first step is to get to Root Directory level (use **CD\**), then key-in:

**MD WORDS**

(MD standing for 'make directory'). If, by coincidence, there happens to be a directory named WORDS already on your disk, a screen message will be displayed saying that the directory cannot be created; in these circumstances, choose another name (note: eight characters are the maximum allowed for a directory name). Then, having created a directory, to convince yourself that it exists, list the Root Directory once again and you will see:

**WORDS**       **<DIR>**

in the listing. Next, go into the WORDS directory and key-in **DIR** to
find out what is listed. In this case only the lines with the full stops
appear because, as yet, no files exist in WORDS.

Volume in drive C IS E DWYER HD20
Directory of C:\WORDS

| | | | | |
|---|---|---:|---|---|
| . | | <DIR> | 28–03–88 | 22:01 |
| .. | | <DIR> | 28–03–88 | 22:01 |
| CHAP0 | TXT | 4480 | 9–04–88 | 14:14 |
| CHAP1 | TXT | 12544 | 19–04–88 | 23:09 |
| CHAP9 | TXT | 24704 | 29–04–88 | 09:01 |
| CHAP3 | TXT | 28544 | 11–05–88 | 11:49 |
| CHAP3 | BAK | 28544 | 11–05–88 | 11:50 |
| CHAP6 | TXT | 45568 | 27–05–88 | 16:56 |
| CHAP4 | TXT | 24960 | 30–05–88 | 09:16 |
| CHAP4 | BAK | 24960 | 30–05–88 | 09:18 |
| CINSTALL | EXE | 15872 | 11–06–84 | 13:13 |
| CORRSTAR | OVR | 59392 | 13–04–88 | 17:10 |
| INTERNAL | DCT | 35584 | 11–06–84 | 19:11 |
| MAIN | DCT | 312320 | 1–01–84 | 20:09 |
| PERSONAL | DCT | 1347 | 11–06–88 | 15:00 |
| WC | EXE | 12288 | 14–06–88 | 20:10 |
| WS | COM | 25600 | 14–06–88 | 20:22 |
| | | | | etc |

            30 File(s)                         15094528 bytes free

**Figure 4.6    A Partial Listing of Files in the WORDS Directory**

**Self-check Activity**

Create two more directories in the Root Directory, namely,
(i) WORDFILE, and (ii) DATABASE.

**Solution**

(i) **MD WORDFILE**     (ii) **MD DATABASE**

This has been a gentle introduction to MS-DOS. You have used CD,

DIR and MD. You have also used the backslash to indicate the Root Directory, and you created three directories with the Root Directory as parent. Quite a lot really. We shall use the directories in later chapters, so hold on to them for the present.

**EXERCISES**

4.1  What happens to data on a disk when it is formatted?

4.2  What are the three advantages of using a hard disk?

4.3  What two steps should be taken to obviate the disadvantages of using a hard disk?

4.4  Create a directory with the name DATAFILE in the Root Directory.

4.5  What is displayed on the screen when you enter DIR from the newly created DATAFILE directory? Try to figure out the answer before you try it out.

4.6  Which option is used with DIR to stop the directory listing scrolling beyond one screen page at any one time?

# Part II

This part starts by looking at ways of improving skills in word processor applications, then goes on to examine the use of MS-DOS to facilitate efficient file management. Approaches to data security are discussed, and the issue is placed in the context of the Data Protection Act.

**Chapter 5: Word Processing**

This chapter focuses on a specific type of applications software package, namely word processing, although much of the content is relevant to other applications. It is first of all concerned with general principles of file management, and examines ways which allow policy to be translated into good practice. The second part of the chapter looks at ways to use a word processor efficiently, and examples from WordStar and WordStar 1512 are used to illustrate recommendations relevant to editing and formatting documents.

**Chapter 6: File Storage and Retrieval**

This chapter looks at MS-DOS in more detail, and after distinguishing between *internal* and *external* MS-DOS commands, it goes on to consider the function of directories. Ways of creating directories are explained, and activities are provided to show how *paths* are used to move around directory *tree structures*.

A detailed account of the internal command COPY is given, followed by instructions on using the commands for displaying files on screen, changing the MS-DOS prompt, renaming files, and deleting files and directories. One external command, FORMAT, is covered, with information on simultaneously copying system command files to provide a *boot-up* disk.

**Chapter 7: Backing-Up and Archiving Files**

This chapter is devoted to the backup commands which are available in MS-DOS, namely COPY, DISKCOPY, BACKUP, RESTORE and XCOPY. All except COPY, which has already been covered in some detail in Chapter 6, are external MS-DOS commands. Apart from some explanations about the ways some of the commands work, the chapter concentrates on their use.

**Chapter 8: Securing Data**

This chapter discusses ways of protecting data against corruption and loss, whether accidental or deliberate. It outlines risks to data, then goes on to consider ways of reducing these risks by preventative measures. Organising backup procedures is presented in terms of archiving and cyclic updating with specific reference in the latter case to the *three-generations* approach to backing-up.

Three approaches to security are described: physical, software and operational, followed by a brief introduction to the Data Protection Act.

# 5 Word Processing

This chapter is specifically about word processors, but certain fundamental data file management principles, which you should try to translate into practice when using applications software in general, are of particular relevance to word processing.

## PRINCIPLES OF FILE MANAGEMENT

Surprisingly, these principles are often overlooked, and when they are file management suffers. They are:

- selecting appropriate filenames;

- placing limits on size of files;

- saving working files regularly;

- purging unwanted files regularly.

### Selecting Appropriate Filenames

Choosing filenames for documents can be a very personal decision undertaken with little thought. You may pick a name which makes sense at the time the document is prepared, but which very often means little to you a couple of months later, and even less to someone else. Filenames, whether you are using a word processor, database, spreadsheet, etc, should therefore be meaningful. Unfortunately, MS-DOS limits a filename to a maximum of eight characters, with an optional extension of a full stop and up to three characters, thus making it impossible to use precisely descriptive filenames for all documents because many would exceed the permitted length. However, a little bit of ingenuity in selecting appropriate abbreviations overcomes this limitation. In addition filenames should be chosen to allow logical connections to be made between sets of filenames.

To take the latter point first, an example of logical connection is found in the way the three characters in the extension allow you to use combinations like .LET for letters, .ADD for addresses, .REP for reports, .DOC for documentations, .INV for invoices, and .MEM for memos, etc. Some software packages create their own filename extensions, particularly databases and spreadsheets. Nothing should be done to change these extensions, otherwise the program will not find the files it is looking for. Database examples are .DBF for data files, and .PRG for program files. There are also some programs which, while they add a default extension, allow you to choose an alternative. For the reasons already given, it is best to take advantage of the facility to use extensions of your own choosing.

Logical connection obviously contributes to meaning, but to ensure that the meanings are recognisable by other users, the full filename should be used to this end: for example, AUDIT88.REP for an auditor's report in 1988, PROFIT87.DOC for the 1987 Profit and Loss account, TAX3.LET for a third letter to the Inland Revenue. Suitable abbreviations, such as BALNCE90.DOC for 1990 balance sheet, can also be used. One small note about filenames: when you edit a file in many word processors, a backup is automatically created with the same filename, but with .BAK as an extension, indicating a backup file. So if you edit a file named BALNCE90.DOC, you will also see BALNCE90.BAK in the list of files after the edited file is saved. (Backup files are treated in some detail in Chapter 7, but it is worth stating here that having a .BAK file could help you in a nasty situation if, for example, you accidentally delete an important file.)

If you follow these simple guidelines on choice of filenames, considerable time will be saved tracking down files, particularly when someone else must do the searching. It would help also to keep a list of all extensions with details of their meanings, and, if practicable, some brief information about the content of files.

## Place Limits on Size of Files

When using a word processor, there is a great temptation to make a file as long as the document you are writing, regardless of document size. In other words, if a document is 50 or more pages in length, it is treated as one file. The word processor makes this so easy it may seem pointless to consider an alternative way of creating files. However, this system is counter-productive because editing long files is very time consuming. The personal computer deals with data in chunks and when files are greater in length than the chunks, the computer swaps text between main memory and disk as you edit, thus adding considerably to the time it takes to process the file. You can imagine the effect this has on searching for a specific part of a file which is not in main memory when the search is initiated.

The simple way to overcome this is to split the document into smaller files, up to about 15 pages at a maximum. The beginning of a file should be where a new page begins in the document, although there is no need to worry unduly about this until all of the document is written. Then adjustments between documents can be made before printing. When saving the files, use appropriate filenames to indicate the order of printouts, SALES1.REP, SALES2.REP, and so on.

When editing is complete, there are different ways to deal with page numbering in the printout. One way is by setting the correct page number at the beginning of each file, or by using the mail-merge facility to join the files at the time of printing. The former approach is a little more time consuming as you have to start the printing of each file manually, but a printer left alone to output a very long document, as when using the mail-merge facility, may deliver a chewed-up mass of paper. If, however, you do not have time to keep an eye on the printer and you have complete trust in it, the mail-merge file-joining approach will speed up operations.

**Save Working Files Regularly**

If your word processor (or any applications software package) does not automatically save your files at regular intervals as you work on them, you should do so yourself. Disaster can strike without warning, for example, your disk drive may cease to function, a power spike may clear the main memory, or a plug may become dislodged and disconnect your computer. All the work you have so diligently completed since last saving it has gone for good, and if a long period has elapsed, much time and effort have been wasted, not to mention what is involved in entering the data all over again. Yet saving the file you are working on at regular intervals will minimise data loss of this type. The duration of the intervals is a matter for yourself to decide. If you do not mind re-entering half-an-hour's work, then half-hourly intervals are fine, but 15 minutes would not inconvenience most people, particularly if files are kept to a reasonable size.

If you are saving to a floppy disk, it is extremely important to keep an eye on the amount of free space available on the disk. To find out how much there is, obtain a file listing for the disk with DIR. The amount of space available is given in bytes at the bottom. As a general rule, if a disk has less than 35,000 bytes free, it is time to exchange it for a fresh one, or at least for a disk with more space. Carry out this check before you enter the word processor, or any application you are about to use. You will be repaid handsomely for the small amount of inconvenience involved because the difficulties associated with running out of disk space arise surprisingly often.

The reason for the emphasis on this point is that you could have problems if the file you wish to save is too long for the disk space available. For example, if in the course of editing an existing file, you increase its size to such an extent that there is not enough free disk space to hold the edited version, any attempt to save it could corrupt the original file. If you are lucky there will be a .BAK version of the file, but do not depend on it in these circumstances. To be on the safe side, it is better if you start by copying the file to a disk which has ample free space, and use this one as a working disk. Remember also that these types of problems are less likely to occur if files are kept to an optimum size.

In addition to saving files, *backing-up* should take place. Backing-up means saving files to another disk, or another medium, so that, by having additional copies, you reduce the chances of losing information. There are two types of backups, *archiving* in which permanent copies of files are made, and *cyclic* backing-up which occurs when backup copies are updated at regular intervals. Because backing-up is so important, Chapter 7 is devoted to the matter, but it is worth pointing out now that backups should be made at least once daily.

### Purge Unwanted Files Regularly

At home, we tend to hold on to all sorts of sundry items which are stored in the roof space or in the garage with a vague hope that some day they will come in useful. Usually we forget all about them. Then a year or two later we have a general clear-out and are never sure what the items were stored for in the first place. The same obsession can drive us to keep a copy of every data file we ever create. This is particularly true for users with hard disks, because it is so easy to store data, and the storage capacity seems to be infinite. The result is that directories become huge 'waste bins' with a tangled web of filenames that renders finding specific files a near-impossible task. In spite of what has been said about the absolute need to back-up data, it is necessary to be ruthless with unwanted files and delete them immediately after their use has been exhausted, or to undertake regular directory purges.

### Self-check Activities

1 What is the simplest means of ensuring that filenames are recognisable?

2 Why is regular saving of a file while you work on it so important?

3 What is a reasonable interval between savings of a working file?

4 What effect does excessive file length have on editing?

5 With hard disks able to hold greater amounts of data, why bother purging unwanted files when there is so much disk space available?

### Solutions

1 Use filenames which are meaningful in relation to the files they are named for.

2 Regular saving means that data loss is insignificant if the computer goes out of action unexpectedly.

3 No more than 30 minutes, although 15 minutes is optimal.

4 It increases the time taken to edit the file.

5 The greater the number of files on a disk, the longer the time to access and process them, so unwanted files merely add to the congestion.

### USING A WORD PROCESSOR WITH GREATER EFFICIENCY

It is probably a truism that just about everyone knows, in general terms, what word processing is. However, as was pointed out in Chapter 3, they are among the least standardised of the applications software packages, but when we consider the many uses word processors are put to, it is not surprising that so many differences have arisen. Their applications range from the production of company reports which include graphic displays, to the drafting of shopping lists in the home; from the composition of manuscripts by authors, to the preparation of assignments by students. It is nevertheless possible to identify certain common functions which all word processors should have. They should allow you to:

- edit text;

- format documents for printing;

- store and retrieve documents;

and for a large number of users there is also a *mail-merge* facility which allows you to:

- merge information from different documents into one document;

- personalise mail;

- print address labels.

A word processor which handles output data from other applications, for example from spreadsheets and databases, and which provides a spelling checker and a thesaurus, is also a useful business asset.

Even the most moderately priced word processors offer an incredibly wide range of facilities, but it is not at all uncommon for many people to use only a small proportion of these features, and therefore leave untapped the full potential of a valuable resource. This is due, in some large extent, to the reluctance of software producers to admit that learning to use their products requires considerable effort. The result is that many users acquire only a minimal competence; just enough to get on with the jobs they do. Indeed, it says much for their ingenuity that they get through so much work with the limited skills they have. There is no suggestion that the newcomer to a particular software package should try to learn everything about it at one go. Acquiring minimal skills is, in fact, an appropriate first step in developing fuller competence; progress can then be made in stages. However, when progress is not made beyond minimal competence, there is a waste of both human and software resources.

The rest of this chapter describes the types of facilities that you should fully exploit in order to increase your efficiency in using a word processor. Although all the features described are those available in WordStar 1512 (and 'standard' WordStar, in nearly all cases), and specific examples, where given, are WordStar 1512 and WordStar functions, most of the content has general application.

('WordStar 1512' is used throughout to refer to the Amstrad-PC-specific applications software package, while 'WordStar' refers to the versions which run on all personal computers. 'Wordstar Express' is similar to WordStar 1512 but runs on non-Amstrad personal computers, so references to the latter also apply to this package.)

## EDITING

Editing is a term which is used differently by different people, but here it means manipulating text in a document until you decide that it is satisfactory. It involves such operations as inserting, moving and deleting text. Most word processor users can edit text with a reasonable degree of efficiency, but some advice is given here on cursor movement, inserting blocks of text, and saving blocks of text.

### Moving Around the Screen

When editing documents, the cursor keys are quite adequate when making short moves. But many users overlook the other keys and key combinations in word processors which allow quick moves around the screen involving greater distances. In WordStar 1512, these are achieved, for example, by using the <Home>, <End>, <Pg Up>, <Pg Dn> and backspace keys, or the <Ctrl> key in combination with these keys. (The procedure in the latter case is to hold down <Ctrl>, then tap the other key. Some examples follow. **Note:** These are for word processing only; the effects of these combinations in MailList (mail-merge) are not quite the same.)

|  | Without the <Ctrl> key | With the <Ctrl> key |
|---|---|---|
| <Home> | go to beginning of line at top of screen page | go to beginning of current line |
| <End> | go to beginning of line at bottom of screen page | go to end of current line |

<**PgUp**>  go to previous screen          go to beginning of
          page                           document

<**PgDn**>  go to next screen page         go to end of document

Using these types of feature will greatly speed up document editing.

**Inserting Blocks**

Many of the business letters you prepare have sections in them which
are repeated in letter after letter. For example, when Joe Bloggs wishes
a correspondent to reply to one of the numerous letters he sends out
weekly, the last line might be 'Please reply to me, Joseph Bloggs, at the
above address, giving full details of your requirements, or telephone me
on Extension 233.' If this were written as a separate document, under
the filename BLOGGS.RPY, it could then be inserted at the appropriate point in all future letters. It does not need much imagination to
realise that this approach will save considerable time and effort if a
number of files, comprising information which is used repeatedly in this
way, are prepared and saved to disk.

**Saving Blocks**

You can imagine how useful it would be if, instead of preparing insert
files individually, you could simply create them by saving a relevant
section of a document you are working on. For example, Joe Bloggs'
letter could be written, and the block in question saved to a separate file
(BLOGGS.RPY). Unfortunately, block saving, although a feature in
WordStar, is not available in WordStar 1512. One way to get round this
omission is, after saving your document, to copy it to another file with
the filename BLOGGS.RPY, which you would: (i) open, (ii) delete all
but the required block, (iii) save the edited version for later use as an
insert file. It could be a bit messy at times, but it does offer a practicable
solution.

**FORMATTING DOCUMENTS**

Formatting a document means preparing it for printing, that is, setting
up margin widths, line spacing, print styles, page lengths, and so on.
This is an entirely different operation from disk formatting. In many
ways, the control which the user has over document formatting is a
measure of the power of the word processor. However, an essential

difficulty which faces all personal computer users is that the screen appearance of a document is not the same as the printed copy. (Quite a number of word processors are projected as WYSIWYG systems, meaning *what you see is what you get*, that is, what you see on the screen is what you get in the printed document; but these claims are questionable.) To take an example, two common font sizes are 10 cpi and 17 cpi (characters per inch), but on screen (unless you use a word processor which uses a graphics mode screen, for example GEM) you will only ever see one font size, whereas in the printout both sizes are displayed, as shown in Figures 5.1 and 5.2.

This degree of differentiation, as illustrated in Figures 5.1 and 5.2, increases in proportion to the number of fonts used, and it is affected also by using the *dot commands* found in WordStar and WordStar 1512 (see next section). However, this should not deter you from making as full use as possible of formatting commands. It is unlikely that you will want to use a range of font sizes anyway, except in relatively short documents where WYSIWYG is not important. If, however, you do decide to go in for fonts in a big way, then you should think of obtaining a fonts software package, or, if you really are enthusiastic, desk-top publishing may be the answer.

```
This is an example of a paragraph written using 10 cpi font.  It
has a larger font than the paragraph below when it appears in the
printout

This is an example of a paragraph written using 17 cpi font.  It
has a smaller font than the paragraph above when it appears in the
printout.
```

**Figure 5.1    Example of Different Font Sizes as They Appear on Screen**

```
This is an example of a paragraph written using 10 cpi font.  It
has a larger font than the paragraph below.

This is an example of a paragraph written using 17 cpi font.  It has a smaller font than the paragraph above.
```

**Figure 5.2    Example of Different Font Sizes as They Appear in the Printout**

**Self-check Activities**

1  When are cursor keys inadequate for editing?

2  What is the difference between saving a file and saving a block?

3  What is the purpose of formatting a document?

**Solutions**

1 Using cursor keys is not suitable when moving more than about three words at a time.

2 Saving a file means saving the entire document you are working on; saving a block means saving a section of the document.

3 To prepare it for printing.

### Boilerplates

Although *boilerplating* is a formatting operation, it has been introduced already in the Editing section on Inserting Blocks, where BLOGGS .RPY is an example. Boilerplates are files or modules which you use many times over, and a word processor is particularly suited to producing them. You can imagine their use for invoice forms, company letter heads, contracts, memos, etc. They are, in effect, files which store a series of formatting commands. (For the curious, the term boiler-plate originated in the American syndicated newspaper industry where typeset copies of articles, prepared on printer's plates, were dispatched to syndicate members for publication.)

### EMBEDDED COMMANDS

Most word processors allow you to include or *embed* commands (codes) in the text of a document during editing. These embedded commands greatly facilitate document formatting. In WordStar they take the form of *dot commands*, that is, a combination of a full stop followed by two letters, then followed in some cases by a set of parameters. It is in the dot command system that WordStar 1512 corresponds very closely to WordStar.

When implemented, dot commands can (during the printing of a document): switch right justification on and off in any part of a document; change margin widths; vary page lengths; insert headers and footers with text at the top and bottom of each page; issue instructions to stop a particular piece of text being split between two pages; etc. Dot commands are, however, among the least used features of WordStar 1512, yet they represent a very powerful facility that can reduce much of the time spent preparing documents which are used repeatedly. In other words, they facilitate boilerplating.

There are fewer than 30 dot commands, and they are relatively easy to remember because they have meanings of a sort. For example, the command to change the size of the left margin is .lm n where n is the margin width in characters; .pl n is page length where n is the number of lines; .pf on/off is the paragraph formatting command which is set to on or off (should be set to on when variations in the paragraph are expected); etc. Because they are embedded in the document, they can be permanently saved, hence their appropriateness for boilerplating. While dot commands are specific to WordStar and WordStar 1512, every word processor worthy of the name has a comparable system. For example, WordPerfect uses *styles*, while Sprint provides *@-sign* commands.

### Making Boilerplates with Dot Commands

Once a boilerplate is set up and saved, it is simply a matter of importing it into the first line of the document being created. Take the example of, say, a hardware catalogue which is regularly updated. It is set out on A4 paper, has a left margin of 10 characters, a line length of 60 characters, a top margin of 6 lines, a header margin of 3 lines, a bottom margin of 7 lines, and a footer of 3 lines. Text in the header is 'Additions to Hardware Catalogue', and text in the footer is 'VAT not included'. A boilerplate with the filename HWARECAT.TEM is then created with these dot commands. (Dot commands must always start in column one, and each is placed on a separate line.)

**.pl 70**      (setting page length for A4, ie 70 lines per page)
**.pf on**      (paragraph formatting on)
**.lm 10**      (left margin 10 characters wide)
**.rm 70**      (line length 60 characters, ie, 70 less left margin)
**.mt 6**       (top margin 6 lines)
**.hm 3**       (header margin 3 lines)
**.mb 7**       (bottom margin 7 lines)
**.fm 3**       (footer margin 3 lines)
**.he Additions to Hardware Catalogue**            (header text)
**.fo VAT not included**                           (footer text)

There is a dot command which imports a file, *.fi filename*. So if the catalogue is being updated for the third time in 1990, HW90–3.CAT is opened and the first line contains the dot command

**.fi HWARECAT.TEM**

This is followed by the updated list.

**Self-check Activities**

1  What is boilerplating particularly suited for?

2  What is the main purpose of WordStar dot commands?

3  What WordStar dot commands would you use for a document with
   the following requirements (assume 10 cpi)? A4 page length; left
   margin 15 characters; line length 55 characters; a header with
   'Building Materials' as text.

**Solutions**

1  For preparing documents which will be used over and over, for
   example, receipts and letters to remind customers of non-payment
   of accounts.

2  To format a document in preparation for printing.

3  **.pl 70**
   **.pf on**
   **.lm 15**
   **.rm 70**
   **.he Building Materials**

**MAIL-MERGE**

*Mail-merge* is a tool for merging documents, but it also enables us to
create files with variables. This simply means that a boilerplate is
created containing sections which are replaced by information from
other files as copies of the boilerplate document are printed. An
example is a letter in which the name and address of the addressee is a
set of variables. Another file exists which holds a list of names and
addresses. When printing starts, each letter imports a name and address
from the list and substitutes them for the set of variables. This continues
until all the names are exhausted.

The mail-merge facility in WordStar 1512 is called MailList, and it
provides a full range of features, including label printing. It has a
decided advantage over WordStar in having a flat file database which
not only feeds information to mail-merge files, but also can be used as a
database in its own right.

**EXERCISES**

5.1 Suggest appropriate filenames for the following documents: (i) a letter to Jones & Sons enquiring about their services, (ii) an invoice to Mr Peter Hammerman, (iii) an annual report, (iv) a job application to Markburys Department Store, (v) a tax return for 1990/91, (vi) an oil prospecting report prepared on three files which will be printed as one document.

5.2 A floppy disk has 12,000 bytes free. On it is a file which you are about to edit. The file is 13,000 bytes. Why should you transfer the file to a new disk before editing?

5.3 What are the consequences of never purging unwanted files?

5.4 What is a .BAK file, and why do some applications software packages create them automatically?

5.5 Describe how you would format a boilerplate document which is used to remind golf club members that their annual subscription is due. There is no need to use dot commands; use descriptive terms such as, left margin 1 inch, page length 66 lines, etc.)

# 6 File Storage and Retrieval

The purpose of this chapter is to expand the information already provided in Chapters 3 and 4 about the operating system, explaining its function by showing how you can use some of its many facilities. However, rather than provide you with a description of all operating system commands, we will concern ourselves with a selection of just a few of the most useful, and look at ways you can apply these with maximum benefit. Having developed competence in these, you should then be able to transfer your newly acquired knowledge to learn the use of other commands independently. In so doing, you will then be able to manage file storage and retrieval on your computer in a way which is not possible with applications software alone.

## INTERNAL AND EXTERNAL MS-DOS COMMANDS

You were introduced to several MS-DOS commands in Chapter 4, and we now go on to look at some others, but before doing so it is important to make a distinction between *internal* and *external* MS-DOS commands. In Chapter 4, it was pointed out that the Root Directory must contain COMMAND.COM and two hidden system files. The hidden files contain the internal MS-DOS commands, hence they do not show in the Root Directory listings. COMMAND.COM acts as an interpreter when you enter an MS-DOS command, checking to see if it is an internal command. If so, it is executed immediately as internal commands are always available regardless of which directory you are in, or which floppy disk you are using at the time, providing you are in MS-DOS, of course. In computer parlance, it is said that the internal commands are *memory resident*, that is, they are placed in main memory at boot-up and remain there until you switch off your computer.

If the command is not internal, COMMAND.COM then checks the external files. Should it still not be found, an error message is displayed on screen. The reason for not being able to find an external command is likely to be that the command file is not on your floppy disk or not in the current directory. External commands appear in directory listings and are easy to recognise by one of the following filename extensions:

.COM

.EXE

.BAT

It is possible that you may have to look for some, or all, of the MS-DOS external command files in a directory other than the hard disk Root Directory, or, if you have floppy disks only, on a different disk from the boot-up disk. If so, this is a likely sign that your disk is well organised because, as was very briefly indicated in Chapter 4, Root Directories should not be cluttered. The same principle should be applied to boot-up floppies. In other words, it may be necessary to change directories or disks to find external MS-DOS commands.

**Note:** With the exception of the MS-DOS internal commands, all command files, whether they are part of MS-DOS or of another software package, use the .COM, .EXE and .BAT extensions, so do not assume that all such files are MS-DOS external commands. In fact, what is said about accessing and activating external MS-DOS commands applies equally to non-MS-DOS commands.

In Chapter 10, you are shown how to set up the system so that external commands can be accessed from any hard disk directory regardless of which directory is current. Your hard disk may already be organised in this way. In this case, the filename of the command may not appear in a listing of the current directory. How then can you tell if a command is an external file if it can be activated but does not appear in the current directory listing? Only by checking your computer manual, although all MS-DOS commands given in this book are identified as internal or external as appropriate.

**Note:** When keying-in a command, the extension is always omitted. However, many require parameters, that is, information required to process the command, such as filename, disk drive and directory.

How you can create your own command programs is shown in

Chapters 9 and 10 where .BAT files (*Batch* files) are covered in more detail.

## USING THE DIRECTORIES

In Chapter 4 you created three directories in the Root Directory, namely WORDS, WORDFILE and DATABASE, and you also created DATAFILE as an end-of-chapter exercise (Exercise 4.4). Figure 6.1 shows the structure of this directory system. These directories are used in the rest of the book for simulation activities. You are not asked to use a word processor or database as such, but you will create small files and use these to undertake exercises in the use of MS-DOS commands. Having done this you can then apply what you have learned when using an application software package. Figure 6.1 is a *tree diagram* (an upside-down tree) in which the Root Directory is the root, and the directories are nodes linked by branches.

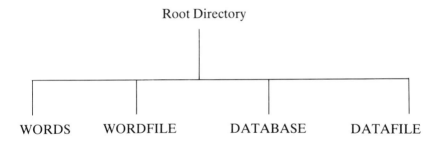

**Figure 6.1 Structure of Directories Created**

### Paths

Viewing the diagram in Figure 6.1 as a tree is a useful starting point for thinking about the purpose of directories, because it suggests that, just as you can climb a tree, you can move about a directory structure by moving up and down its branches. This is exactly what you do, and it is accomplished by using a *path* as you go from one directory to another. You have already been using paths, for example, when you used the command CD\ to move to the Root Directory. The backslash coming immediately after the command indicates the Root Directory. So, at this stage, boot-up your computer, and move to the WORDS directory by keying-in:

### CD\WORDS

that is, go to the Root Directory (indicated by CD\), then to WORDS. Next, go from WORDS to WORDFILE. Do this by keying-in:

### CD\WORDFILE

that is, go back to the Root Directory, then on to WORDFILE. The implication is that you cannot jump straight to WORDFILE from WORDS by using CD WORDFILE; you must go back to the root of the tree, so to speak, and then up a different branch, or path.

### Self-check Activity

If you are in WORDS, which commands do you key-in to go to (i) DATABASE, and (ii) DATAFILE?

### Solution

(i) **CD\DATABASE**    (ii) **CD\DATAFILE**

If you are already in the Root Directory, there is no need to enter the backslash immediately after the command, so to go to WORDS, CD WORDS is sufficient. However, the good news is that putting in the backslash does not invalidate the command, provided that the directory you wish to go to has the Root Directory as a parent. Later in the chapter, paths which start from other directories are described.

The purpose of using paths (moving between directories) is to use the files which are resident in the different directories. You have already discovered this to some extent in Chapter 3 when you moved to the Root Directory and issued the DIR command. The result was a display of the listing of the directories and files in the Root Directory only. To get a listing of another directory, you go there first (although this must be qualified as the paths can be used to issue commands in directories other than the one you are in, but we will leave that for later).

Although this use of DIR does indicate the way paths are used, it is not an appropriate example because DIR, being an internal MS-DOS command, is available in all directories, and to all disks. However, to issue a command which is available only in another directory, go to the directory first, then key-in the command. For example, assume that you have a word processor in WORDS, say WordStar, which is activated by keying-in WS. The steps are:

**CD\WORDS**
**WS**

**Note:** WS.EXE is part of the WordStar application program, not MS-DOS. If you are using WordStar 1512, you would, of course, enter WS1512 for the WS1512.EXE command. However, the installation program for WordStar 1512 places the WS1512.EXE command in the Root Directory, so there is no need to change to the WordStar 1512 directory in this case.

### Self-check Activity

What are the paths for (i) WORDFILE, (ii) DATABASE, and (iii) DATAFILE?

### Solution

    (i) **\WORDFILE**   (ii) **\DATABASE**   (iii) **\DATAFILE**

When you finish working in WordStar, the file is saved in the WORDS directory. To transfer the file from WORDS to WORDFILE the COPY command is used. (COPY is an internal MS-DOS command.)

### COPY

To show you how to use COPY, you will first need to create a short file, MYNAME.DOC, in the WORDS directory, then copy it to the WORDFILE directory. This operation simulates what would happen if your word processor were in WORDS. The first step is to go into the WORDS directory and key-in:

    **COPY CON MYNAME.DOC**

The option CON tells the computer that you want to copy a file entered from the keyboard (console), and MYNAME.DOC is the name of the file you wish to create. When you press <Return>, after keying-in the command, the cursor moves to the next line and waits for you to enter data. At this stage, write your name, then finish off by pressing <Return>, then key-in:

    **<F6>**

followed by <Return>. ˆZ appears on the screen when you press

<F6>, indicating the end of the file. Then when you press <Return> after <F6>, the file is saved in the WORDS directory.

To check that COPY CON has been successful, key-in:

**TYPE MYNAME.DOC**

and what you keyed-in (other than the COPY CON line, and ^Z) appears on the screen. TYPE is an internal command which displays the file contents on the screen. The form is:

**TYPE [d:] [\path] filename**

The square brackets indicate an option. d: is the drive letter, and, if omitted, the current drive is assumed. \path is used if you wish to activate a file in a directory other than the current directory, and the current directory is assumed if omitted. However, both the current drive and directory may be included.

Next we copy a file from one directory to another, but before doing this, let us examine the full form of the COPY command:

**COPY [CON] [s:][\path] filename [t:][\path] [filename]**

s: indicates the disk drive on which the file to be copied exists (*source* drive), and if omitted assumes the current drive; t: indicates the disk drive to which the file is copied (*target* drive), and, as before, indicates the current drive if omitted. (s and t to indicate drives are used throughout the book where two drives are implicated, as when copying files from disk to disk, and d where one drive only is involved.) However, do not concern yourself with the details of the form of COPY. The examples below make its meaning clear, but you can always come back to it for reference.

To copy MYNAME.DOC to the WORDFILE directory, key-in:

**COPY MYNAME.DOC \WORDFILE\MYNAME.DOC**

**Note:** COPY leaves the original file in place; it does not remove it from the WORDS directory.

Something new in this command is the second backslash (after WORDFILE). This time it does not refer to the Root Directory. A backslash refers to the Root Directory only when it comes immediately to the left of the parameters, whether they be the source parameters (MYNAME.DOC in this case) or destination parameters (\WORD-

FILE\MYNAME.DOC). Here, the second backslash is used as a separator between the directory name and the filename, and it indicates a branch of the tree pointing to a lower level. It is similarly used to separate a directory from its subdirectory.

In fact, there is no need to include the destination filename unless you wish to change it, so:

**COPY MYNAME.DOC \WORDFILE**

is sufficient. If, however, you wish to change the filename when you copy the file to the WORDFILE directory, say to NAME.DOC, then insert \NAME.DOC immediately after \WORDFILE, as follows:

**COPY MYNAME.DOC \WORDFILE\ NAME.DOC**

To copy MYNAME.DOC from WORDS to the Root Directory, the command is:

**COPY MYNAME.DOC \**

Only the backslash is required for the Root Directory. If you wish to rename the file as NAME.DOC in the Root Directory, then key-in:

**COPY MYNAME.DOC \NAME.DOC**

**Note:** If the filename you are copying already exists in the destination directory, the existing file is overwritten by the incoming file.

Now create a second file, MYADDR.DOC. Use COPY CON again, and write your address when you open the file. (It is necessary to use <Return> to go to a new line, unlike a word processor using line wrap.)

**Self-check Activities**

1 What commands are used (i) to copy MYADDR.DOC to the WORDFILE directory, (ii) to copy MYADDR.DOC as ADDRESS.DOC to the WORDFILE directory?

2 How do you check that the files in 1 have been copied?

3 When does the backslash in a path refer to the Root Directory?

**Solutions**

1 (i)   **COPY MYADDR.DOC \WORDFILE**

  (ii) **COPY MYADDR.DOC \WORDFILE\ADDRESS.DOC**

2 Change to the WORDFILE directory, and use the TYPE command with both files.

3 The backslash refers to the Root Directory when it is located prior to the parameter(s), as, for example, in:

**COPY MYADDR.DOC \WORDFILE \ADDRESS.DOC**

the backslash immediately to the left of WORDFILE indicates the Root Directory, that is, the path starting at the Root Directory; the backslash immediately to the left of ADDRESS.DOC is a separator (or branch).

Having gone through these examples, it is now relatively easy to see how files are copied from WORDS to WORDFILE, and from DATABASE to DATAFILE, or any file from any directory to any other directory. Paths also allow you to copy files from one disk drive to another by entering the drive at the beginning of the filename or directory path. For example, if you have two floppy drives and you wish **to copy MYNAME.DOC from WORDS in drive A to in drive B, then key-in:**

**COPY A:MYNAME.DOC B:**

You may omit A: if A is the current drive, so if you wish to copy MYNAME.DOC as NAME.DOC in drive B:, then key-in:

**COPY MYNAME.DOC B:NAME.DOC**

There is no backslash this time as it is assumed that there is only one directory on disk B.

If you have a hard disk (drive C) and wish to copy MYNAME.DOC from drive A (the current drive) to WORDFILE in C, then key-in:

**COPY MYNAME.DOC C:\WORDFILE**

**Using Paths with COPY**

It is also possible to use paths to copy from directories other than the current directory. For example, if you are in WORDFILE, and wish to copy MYNAME.DOC from WORDS to DATAFILE, then key-in:

**COPY\WORDS\ MYNAME.DOC \DATAFILE**

**Self-check Activities**

1 (i) Go to the Root Directory, (ii) copy MYNAME.DOC from

WORDS to DATABASE as NAME.DOC.

2 (i) Go to the DATABASE directory, (ii) copy MYNAME.DOC from WORDS to DATABASE as NAME.DOC.

**Solutions**

1 (i) **CD\**

(ii) **COPY\ WORDS\MYNAME.DOC \DATABASE\ NAME.DOC**

2 (i)  **CD\DATABASE**

(ii) **COPY\WORDS\MYNAME.DOC NAME.DOC**

**Note:** Obviously, this use of paths saves time, but there is a need to be careful that your paths do not become too long as complexity increases the possibility of making errors.

**WordStar 1512 Directories**

The installation of WordStar 1512 causes a directory system to be set up as shown in Figure 6.2. The files created by WordStar 1512 are stored in TEXT. So if you write MYNAME.DOC with WordStar 1512, and wish to copy it to drive A, the command is:

**COPY\1512\TEXT\ MYNAME.DOC A:**

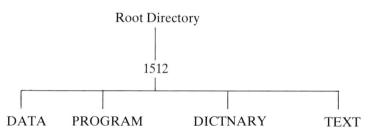

**Figure 6.2    WordStar 1512 Directories**

**Copying Groups of Files**

There is a very convenient feature in MS-DOS which lets us handle groups of related filenames using *wildcard* symbols. It is best to explain this with an example using the two files already created, MYNAME.DOC and MYADDR.DOC. We can take advantage of their common extension, .DOC, by substituting the wildcard symbol * for MYNAME and MYADDR, that is *.DOC, which means 'any filename with the extension .DOC'. So by keying-in:

**COPY *.DOC \DATABASE**

all files with the .DOC extension in the current directory are copied to DATABASE. If there were a large number of such files, you can see that the wildcard would catch all in its net. This facility saves considerable time when dealing with groups of files and is another reason for standardising filename extensions as recommended in Chapter 5.

If you are copying all files across directories or disks, then the wildcard symbol takes the form *.*, for example, to copy all files from floppy disk A to the current hard disk directory (say, WORDS), key-in:

**COPY A:*.***

If you are not in the WORDS directory, then the path must be included:

**COPY A:*.* \WORDS**

Copying in the reverse direction follows the same pattern, and is particularly important because this is one way of backing-up several files with a single command. So assuming you are in the WORDFILE directory, the command is:

**COPY *.* A:**

but if you are in a different directory, the command is:

**COPY\WORDFILE\*.* A:**

Finally, if you were in the A disk, and you wished to copy (i) all files from the WORDFILE directory on drive C, and (ii) all files from drive B, key-in:

(i) **COPY C:\WORDFILE\*.***

(ii) **COPY B:*.***

**Note:** When copying within the same directory or disk, the destination filename must be different from the source filename.

**Self-check Activities**

1  What command is used to copy MYNAME.DOC from WORDS to WORDFILE (i) if the current drive is C and the current

directory is DATAFILE, (ii) if the current drive is A?

2  What is wrong with **COPY\WORDS\MYNAME.DOC \WORDS?**

**Solutions**

1  (i)   **COPY\WORDS\ MYNAME.DOC \WORDFILE**

   (ii)  **COPY C:\WORDS\MYNAME.DOC C:\WORDFILE**

**Note:** The solution in (ii) could also be used in (i).

2  You cannot copy a file on to itself. For this COPY command to be successfully executed, the file has to be copied to another filename, or to another directory.

## PROMPT

PROMPT refers to the internal command which alters the content of the MS-DOS screen prompt. One of the most useful prompt messages displays the current directory and you are shown how to do this below. However, first change the prompt in your machine to display the drive letter only. To do this, key-in:

### PROMPT

The result is a prompt showing **A>**, **B>** or **C>**, according to your current drive. It may have been like this already, but no matter. Now key-in:

### PROMPT I love MS-DOS

The prompt changes to **I love MS-DOS**. So, as you can see, you may enter any text message as part of the prompt, but to obtain a prompt which displays the current directory, go to the WORDS directory (if you are not already there), then key-in:

### PROMPT $P$G

The prompt now displays **C:\WORDS>** (or **A:\WORDS>**). There are other parameters which allow you to customise the prompt, for example:

**$D**     displays the date;

**$T**     displays the time;

**$V**     displays the MS-DOS version.

In Chapter 10, you are shown how to install a prompt so that it appears automatically after boot-up.

## OTHER MS-DOS COMMANDS

While we have looked at only a small number of MS-DOS commands, namely MD, CD, DIR, COPY, TYPE and PROMPT, the information provided has general application, particularly in relation to paths. So, while some other commands are listed, no detailed information is provided, but you should try them out.

**Deleting Files    DEL** (internal command)

> **DEL [d:][\][path\]filename**

To delete MYNAME.DOC:

> **DEL C:\WORDS\MYNAME.DOC**

is the full command. If you are in the WORDS directory, **DEL MYNAME.DOC** will do the job, but if you are not quite sure which paths to include or omit, incorporate the lot until you are more confident.

**Note:** If the purpose of copying a file is to move it to a different directory altogether, and not just create a duplicate, the file should be deleted from the source directory immediately after it has been copied to the destination directory.

If you wish to delete all files in a directory, the format is:

> **DEL [d:][\][path\]*.\***

You are then asked **Are you sure (Y/N)?** to give you a chance to consider the effects of this instruction.

**Deleting Directories    RD** (internal command)

> **RD [d:][\][path\]directory-name**

Before this command (Remove Directory) can be successfully executed, there must be no files in the directory.

**Renaming Files    REN** (internal command)

> **REN [d:][\][path\]old-filename new-filename**

**Formatting Disks   FORMAT** (external command)

**FORMAT [d:][option]**

This is the first example of an external MS-DOS command you have been asked to execute, so remember that you may have to change directories to find and execute it. You can try keying-in the command as instructed, and if it is not accessible in the current directory, an error message will be displayed on screen, namely, 'Bad command or file name'. In this case you will have to look for the file in another directory or on another disk.

First, a word of warning: while there is no harm in practising formatting floppy disks, **do not format the hard disk** unless it is essential, but, should it be necessary, make sure that you have made floppy copies of all the files on it beforehand, so that you can copy these back when formatting is complete.

The next step now is to let you actually format a floppy disk. First, get a new floppy disk, or a used one holding information that you do not need. If you have two floppy drives, put the disk to be formatted into drive B, then, **making sure you include the drive letter and colon**, key-in:

**FORMAT B:**

and press <Return>.

If you have a single floppy drive only, or a hard disk (with a single floppy drive), put the disk to be formatted in drive A, and **making sure you include the drive letter and colon**, key-in:

**FORMAT A:**

and press <Return>.

Then follow the instructions about inserting disks which appear on screen. When the formatting is complete, a message asking you if you wish to format another disk is displayed. Key-in **N** (for no).

A very useful option which can be used with FORMAT copies COMMAND.COM and the two hidden system files to the disk being formatted. This means that you can use the newly formatted disk to boot-up the computer. The option is /S which is included in the command as follows:

**FORMAT [d:]/S**

for example,

**FORMAT A:/S**

## A FURTHER LOOK AT PATHS

It is good policy to keep your directory system broad and shallow. This means you should not have more than one or two generations of subdirectories, thus avoiding complex paths. Nevertheless, by way of explanation, we shall add a lower level by creating LETTERS in WORDFILE. There are two ways to do this:

**CD\WORDFILE**
**MD LETTERS**

or,

**MD\WORDFILE\LETTERS**

### Self-check Activity

How would you create another directory in WORDFILE named INVOICES?

### Solution

INVOICES is created in the same way as LETTERS, namely:

**CD\WORDFILE**
**MD INVOICES**

or,

**MD\WORDFILE\INVOICES**

The tree diagram in Figure 6.3 shows the additional level of directories. If the Root Directory is the current directory, to change to LETTERS, key-in:

**CD\WORDFILE\LETTERS**

If WORDS is the current directory, to copy MYNAME.DOC from WORDS to LETTERS, key-in:

**COPY MYNAME.DOC\WORDFILE\ LETTERS**

If the Root Directory is the current directory, to copy MYNAME.DOC from WORDS to LETTERS, key-in:

**COPY\WORDS\ MYNAME.DOC \WORDFILE\LETTERS**

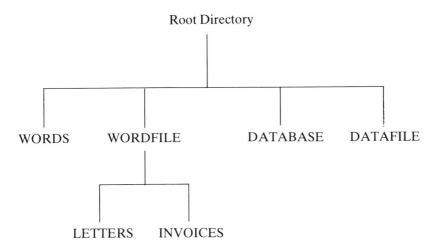

**Figure 6.3    Structure of Directories with Lower Level Subdirectories**

**Self-check Activity**

What command is required to copy MYNAME.DOC to the LETTERS directory with the filename NAME.DOC?

**Solution**

**COPY\ WORDS\MYNAME.DOC \WORDFILE\ LETTERS\NAME.DOC**

**Path Formats – Summary**

1 A backslash which immediately follows the MS-DOS command indicates the Root Directory, for example:

**CD\WORDS**

2 A backslash which comes immediately to the left of the first directory or filename indicates the Root Directory, for example, if you are in WORDS:

**COPY MYNAME.DOC \WORDFILE**

3 A backslash between directory names, or between directory and filename, is a separator to indicate a branch, or to put it more simply, it divides a directory from its subdirectory, or a directory from a file, for example:

**COPY MYNAME.DOC \WORDFILE\NAME.DOC**

**Note:** The backslash divides a directory from its own subdirectory, not from a subdirectory which is located in some other directory. To get to a 'foreign' subdirectory, it is necessary to start from the Root Directory and trace a way through the paths of the appropriate branches of the directory tree.

**EXERCISES**

6.1 What is the difference between an internal and external MS-DOS command file?

6.2 Which of the following commands are internal, and which are external: (i) COPY, (ii) DEL, (iii) FORMAT, (iv) DIR, (v) PROMPT?

6.3 Why can you be sure that you can execute an internal command from any MS-DOS command line?

6.4 If the current drive is C, what command do you enter to view the contents of floppy disk A, without leaving C?

6.5 If the current drive is A, what command do you enter to view the contents of the INVOICES directory in C, without leaving A?

6.6 If the current directory is DATAFILE in drive C, what command is necessary to move to INVOICES?

6.7 Assuming the directory structure shown in Figure 6.4 what are the paths required to reach A1 from the following starting points: (i) Root Directory, (ii) C, (iii) A, (iv) A2, (v) B2?

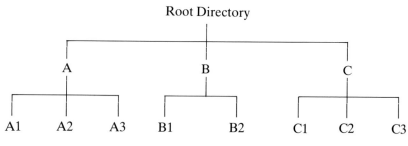

**Figure 6.4    Directory Structure**

# 7 Backing-Up and Archiving Files

Microcomputers have become extremely reliable in recent years, so we tend to forget that faults will inevitably develop, as they do in any machine. The consequences of not being prepared for system failure could be the harmful disruption of data processing activities essential to the smooth running of a business. Particularly grave would be the effects of a hard disk breakdown which resulted in the complete loss of crucial information. The only way to avoid disasters of this kind is to take regular backup copies of all files essential for the continuance of the business. This means creating copies of the files on separate disks which are then stored away from the computer. Indeed, backing-up data should be a daily routine (at least) for anyone using a microcomputer in any enterprise which depends on the reliable storage and retrieval of information. How to organise backup systems is discussed in Chapter 8 where data security in general is covered, but in this chapter the techniques of backing-up are described.

## HARDWARE DEVICES FOR TAKING BACKUPS

There are hardware systems which provide backup solutions, the most common being high capacity tape drives which house removable cassettes. These devices simply store data sequentially and are convenient for making backup copies of all files. If speed of retrieval is an issue, tape cartridge systems may be a better although more expensive solution. There is also the Bernoulli drive which is a removable hard disk system, and which may replace the fixed hard disk drive in the future. The prospect of optical reading systems such as compact discs is becoming more of a reality now, but here it is assumed that you do not have any add-on hardware storage devices for taking backups, and that your backups are to be created on floppy disks. This chapter, therefore, deals entirely with software solutions to backing-up on floppy disks, and is concerned only with MS-DOS facilities which you already have.

## BACKING-UP USING MS-DOS

The importance of making backups cannot be over-emphasised, particularly if you have a hard disk machine. Indeed, the need to back-up data is rooted in the nature of hard disks; their huge storage capacity affords optimum opportunity to have maximum damage inflicted on your data when breakdowns occur. The situation is not nearly so serious with floppy disks because the amount of data which can be lost is relatively small in comparison, and being able to remove disks from the drive also reduces the likelihood of data loss. There is a school of thought which recommends that all data on a hard disk machine should be routed to drive A anyway, thus avoiding the effects of hard disk failure. Nevertheless, if the only copies are on floppy disks it is imperative to make backup copies of these as well.

How can you know which files to back-up? To answer this question let us look at a way of categorising files. We then use the categories to consider the most appropriate approach to making backups. Two general categories can be identified: program software (including systems software and applications software) and data files.

### Program Software

The answer to the backup question as far as program software is concerned is simple. Always make backups! As soon as possible after obtaining applications software, including any software packages which were included with your computer when it was purchased, you should make floppy disk copies of each disk received, unless you bought copy-protected software (fortunately, software houses are abandoning the unhelpful practice of copy-protecting disks). Do this as soon as possible if you have not done so already. Should you possess a machine without a hard disk, put the original disks away safely, and use the backup copies as your working disks.

If you have a hard disk you should also make backups of applications software on floppies as well as copying to the hard disk; you can then use these backups to re-install an application if the need arises. In other words, avoid using the originals other than for creating backups, and if a working backup is accidentally erased or becomes corrupted, your first action should be to make a replacement backup. Having made backups, a disaster will not result if a program is accidentally lost or corrupted.

Systems software disks should also be backed-up, and hard disk users should consider making copies of systems software after it is installed, then, should a major file loss occur, you can simply copy the system files back into their directories without having to call on installation procedures. The same approach can be adopted for applications software.

**Note**: Program disks should have the *write-protect* notch covered with a sticker. The notch is a small square 'bite' on the left side of a 5.25 inch disk (looking at the disk as it is inserted into the drive). Stickers are always supplied with blank disks. When you have completed backing-up a program disk, cover the notch on the backup disk as well. Write-protecting a 3.5 inch disk is carried out by pushing a little built-in slide into position. It is located on the bottom right corner of the disk. Once a disk is write-protected, no-one is able to overwrite it (unless the sticker is removed or slide pulled back).

However, data files present the greatest challenge for backup management. Applications software packages do not change, and backing-up therefore is a straightforward matter of copying the master disks when purchased, or the files when installed. But many applications generate data files which are either being constantly updated, or being added to, and so require a different approach to backup.

### Data Files

A data file is a collection of data rather than a program. Unlike the program software which never changes, many data files undergo continual modification and updating, and therefore require constant backing-up to ensure that up-to-date information is available in the event of a data loss. You should back-up on at least one occasion daily (this issue is discussed in Chapter 8).

It is of particular importance to back-up updated versions of databases, spreadsheets and accounts software, and while it may be less applicable to files created by word processors, it depends on the nature of the document being produced. Reports which are prepared well in advance of publication but which will be altered as changes in business circumstances take place, are examples of updating documents created by word processors.

On the other hand, letters to customers, memos, circulars, etc, once written, are seldom changed. They may be modified to produce different documents, but in these cases the modifications are distinct from the originals. Where it is important to keep any of these files as records of transactions, backups should be made. This is known as *archiving*, that is, placing copies of files in permanent storage, leaving them untouched unless a reason arises to resurrect them. However, files which are not important, or which have been stored as written copies (*hard* copies), should be removed from the disk. As you saw in Chapter 5, you need to be ruthless about this. The vast amount of storage space on a hard disk tempts us to save every document, leaving an unmanageable collection of files which take up disk space unnecessarily and slow down access considerably.

**MS-DOS COMMANDS FOR TAKING BACKUPS**

There are several commands in MS-DOS which are used for taking backups. Each is useful for a particular backup application. We examine them in turn, starting with the internal command, COPY, then look at the external commands, DISKCOPY, BACKUP, RESTORE and XCOPY.

**COPY**

The COPY command is one of the most useful of the utilities for backup operations. It is covered in some detail in Chapter 6 so there is no need to dwell on it further except to clarify its use in backup operations. To start with, a word of warning: it should not be used as the main backup procedure in a business unless your file productivity level is very low. However, you will find it particularly suitable if, for example, you are working on a long document which is broken into sections, each saved as a separate file.

Many software application packages access the COPY command from within the application. They do not, however, all give access to the full range of facilities available in COPY, and what is on offer differs from package to package. Generally speaking, the more sophisticated the package, the fuller the range of facilities.

Finally, do not forget to check that there is sufficient free space on your backup disk before using COPY. This point was discussed in Chapter 5, but it is worth mentioning again because of its importance.

## DISKCOPY

DISKCOPY is an external MS-DOS command, so you may have to change directories, or disks, to activate it. In a directory listing, it is recognisable as DISKCOPY.COM (or DISKCOPY.EXE), so a search will locate it for you. This advice applies to other external command files considered in this chapter, and elsewhere in the book.

The DISKCOPY command copies from and to floppy disks only, but is the most convenient way to take backup copies of master program disks as it makes an exact copy of a source disk on a destination disk. It takes the form:

### DISKCOPY s: t:

where s is the source drive and t the target drive. If you have twin drives, the operation is straightforward, s is A: and t is B: (or vice versa), but if you have a single floppy drive (even with a hard disk), you nominate both s and t as A:. Then, during the actual copying, MS-DOS continually prompts you to exchange source and target disks. (In fact, with a single floppy drive, it does not matter if you nominate the drives as A and B because MS-DOS reacts in the correct manner anyway.)

However, DISKCOPY should be restricted to program disks as there are inherent disadvantages in its use. Because it makes an exact copy, any unused or corrupted areas on the source disk find their way to the destination disk. This does not matter with program disks, providing, of course, that the program files are not corrupted, but it is very wasteful on backup disk space when data files are involved.

## BACKUP

BACKUP is a utility specifically for creating backups and was introduced to cope with hard disks, but it saves files in a special format which must be restored with the RESTORE command before they can be used (see section below for details on RESTORE). The advantage of using BACKUP compared with COPY and DISKCOPY is that it gives you considerable control with minimal effort over the way files are selected for backup, and the way backup is effected. You can, for example, set BACKUP to copy only those files which you have created or modified since the previous backup, or since a specified date or time. These controls are exercised by inserting options, or switches, in the BACKUP command. The number of options available depends on which version of MS-DOS you have.

Using BACKUP also removes the need to check on the amount of space available on backup disks; when a destination disk fills, BACKUP prompts for a replacement, so the size of files being copied is immaterial. However, if your copy of MS-DOS is earlier than Version 3.3, the backup disks, if new, must be formatted beforehand. With the earlier versions, if you run out of formatted disks, you will have to start the entire process again after breaking off to get your disks ready. The form of the command is:

**BACKUP s: [\path][filename] t: [option][option]…**

BACKUP command options (note the differences between earlier and later versions of MS-DOS):

| | |
|---|---|
| **/A** | add the files to those on the backup disk |
| **/D:dd-mm-yy** | back-up files created or changed since the date indicated |
| **/M** | back-up only the files which have been created or modified since the previous backup |
| **/S** | back-up files in the subdirectories also |
| **/L** | create a file, BACKUP.LOG, which is stored in the Root Directory and which logs the names of the backed-up files (the backed-up files' names are appended to BACKUP.LOG) – introduced in Version 3.1 |
| **/T:hh:mmx** | back-up files created or changed since time indicated (**x** refers to **p** for pm, or **a** for am) – introduced in Version 3.1 |
| **/F** | format backup disk if necessary – introduced in Version 3.3. |

Other differences: Versions 2 allow only backups from a hard disk to a floppy disk; Versions 3 allow backups from a floppy disk to another floppy disk, a floppy to a hard disk, a hard disk to another directory on itself, or a hard disk to another hard disk.

A simple BACKUP command from the Root Directory is:

**BACKUP C: A:/S**

that is, back-up to drive A all files on hard disk C. When you back-up for the first time you could be in for a long wait; about an hour if there are lots of files on drive C. It is undesirable anyway to back-up an entire hard disk. Backups should be taken at directory level in most cases, and wildcards can be used to organise backups. For example, to back-up all files with the extension .DOC in the WORDFILE directory, the command is:

**BACKUP C:\WORDFILE\*.DOC A:**

Even if the first backup is a lengthy affair, very little time is required thereafter if you repeat the operation daily using the /M and /A options, as only files worked on during the course of the day are copied.

There are, nevertheless, conditions which must be observed when using the /M and /A options. If the BACKUP command contains /M but not /A, all existing files on the destination disk are wiped before backup takes place. In this situation a warning is displayed on screen informing you that the target disk will be erased. Using /A prevents this. However, /A cannot be used in the first backup; in other words, a backup file must already be on the target disk beforehand. But after that, always include /A to prevent losing the earlier backups. For example, if you write several letters which you wish to back-up, assuming their extensions are .LET and they are in the WORDS directory, the first backup command is:

**BACKUP C:\WORDS\*.LET A:/M**

(/M is optional here.) Thereafter, the /A option must be included:

**BACKUP C:\WORDS\*.LET A:/M/A**

The function of BACKUP is to deal with new or modified data and not with program files (which should already have been backed-up using COPY or DISKCOPY). The directory structure advocated in Chapter 6 would accommodate the most efficient use of BACKUP as it could be used specifically to backup files in directories such as WORDFILE and DATAFILE (see Figure 6.1). It is interesting to note that this type of directory system is a built-in feature of WordStar 1512, with all data files being stored in the TEXT directory. So, if you use a hard disk, by issuing the command:

**BACKUP C:\1512\TEXT A:/M/A**

at the end of each day, you can be sure that only newly created and modified WordStar 1512 documents are saved. (If you have MS-DOS Version 3.2, you should also log them with the /L option.)

If you use another word processor, such as WordStar, the structure displayed in Figure 6.1 would enable you to back-up as follows. First, ensure that all the modified or newly created files have filenames which relate to the document content. For example, .LET for letters, .INV for invoices, and .PER for personal documents. Secondly, at backup time, copy the files into the WORDFILE directory, for example:

**COPY \WORDS\*.LET \WORDFILE**

and so on. Then backup the entire directory, for example:

**BACKUP C:\WORDFILE\*.* A:/M/A**

How does BACKUP know which files have been modified? It is very simple really. In Chapter 4, you saw how disks are organised. Part of the organisation consists of the creation of a table which holds information about files, such as filenames, size of files, date and time of creation of files. All of this information is displayed on screen after DIR is keyed-in. In addition, the table also contains a list of each file's attributes which represent one of a range of properties rather like light switches; that is, they are either on or off. For example, whether a file is *hidden* or not, or if it is *read only* or *read and write*. One of these properties is the *archive* attribute which is set to on when a file is created or modified. BACKUP with the /M option copies only files with the archive switch set to on. Having copied the file, BACKUP turns the switch to off, and so ignores the file when BACKUP is next issued (unless the file has been modified in the meantime).

**Note:** Do not confuse *archiving* in relation to backing-up files, and *archive* which refers to file attributes.

Now, with reference to the directory structure illustrated in Figure 6.3, we can use BACKUP with files in the WORDFILE directory. First of all, go into WORDFILE and create three new files, namely, NEWFILE1.LET, NEWFILE2.LET and NEWFILE3.LET, by copying an existing file to these filenames (refer to the section on COPY in Chapter 6 if you have forgotten how to do this), or by using COPY CON. Next, place a formatted, blank floppy disk in drive A, if you have a hard disk, or in drive B, if you have twin floppy drives, and key-in:

**BACKUP *.LET A:**

(Use drive B in place of A where appropriate.) Check the directory listing on the target drive to convince yourself that the operation has been successful. What you see in the listing will depend on the version of MS-DOS you have. Next, create another file with the .LET extension. If you copy from another file, do not use a .LET file as the source because the archive attribute will now be set to off, and the /M option in the next BACKUP command will cause the file to be disregarded. Should you be unsure about this, create another .LET file with COPY CON. Having created the new file, key-in:

**BACKUP *.LET A:/M/A**

(Use drive B in place of A where appropriate.) The /M option allows only new or modified files to be copied, and the /A option prevents the existing backups from being overwritten, and adds the new file to those already backed-up. Any further backups you take should therefore include both options.

**Self-check Activities**

1 With reference to the directory structure illustrated in Figure 6.3, go into LETTERS and, using COPY CON, create a new file, DOSTEST1.LTR, to contain the message 'I am getting very fond of MS-DOS'. Then create two further files by copying DOSTEST1.LTR to DOSTEST2.LTR and DOSTEST3.LTR. Next, BACKUP these files, using the wildcard character in the parameters, to a clean, formatted backup floppy disk.

2 Using COPY CON, create an extra file, DOSTEST4.LTR, with the same message as before. Next move to the Root Directory and BACKUP the .LTR files to the backup disk. Use the appropriate BACKUP options so that only the new file is copied.

**Solutions**

1 **BACKUP *.LTR A:** (B: in place of A: as appropriate.)
2 **BACKUP \WORDFILE\LETTERS\*.LTR A:/M/A**
(B: in place of A: as appropriate.)

**RESTORE**

Before you can use files copied with BACKUP you must first RESTORE them. The form of the command is:

**RESTORE s: t:[\path][filename][option][option]**...

where s: is the backup disk, and t: the target or working disk.

RESTORE command options are as follows (note the differences between earlier and later versions of MS-DOS:

| | |
|---|---|
| **/P** | prompt for permission to restore read-only files or files which were modified since last backup |
| **/S** | restore files in the subdirectories also |
| **/L:hh:mmx** | restore files created or changed on or after time indicated (**x** refers to **p** for pm, and **a** for am) – introduced in Version 3.1 |
| **/M** | restore only the files which have been changed or deleted since the previous backup – introduced in Version 3.1 |
| **/N** | restore only those files which are no longer on the destination disk – introduced in Version 3.1 |
| **/A:dd-mm-yy** | restore only the files created or changed on or after the date indicated – introduced in Version 3.1 |
| **/B:dd-mm-yy** | restore only the files created or changed on or before the date indicated – introduced in Version 3.1 |
| **/E:hh:mmx** | restore files created or changed on or before time indicated (**x** refers to **p** for pm, or **a** for am) – introduced in Version 3.1. |

**Note:** For BACKUP and RESTORE to work correctly, you should use the same version of MS-DOS for both, and the same paths and filenames for both. However, using the /P option will give you the chance to prevent the read-only system files from an earlier version of MS-DOS from being written over files from a later version. Indeed it is a good idea to use the /P option with RESTORE at all times.

When you enter the RESTORE command you are prompted for the first backup disk. If you have more than one, insert them in the drive in the same order as the original BACKUP sequence. As an example of RESTORE, we can use the backups of the files in LETTERS (see 1 in the last Self-check Activities). If you wish to check that RESTORE is successful after execution, then delete the original files first. Next place the backup disk in A (or B as appropriate) and key-in:

**RESTORE A: C:\WORDFILE\ LETTERS/P**

or,

**RESTORE B: A:\WORDFILE\ LETTERS/P**

If you do not wish to restore all the backed-up files, specific files may be nominated, or wildcards used with RESTORE. In this case, it is necessary to specify the filenames in the destination parameters, for example, to restore .LET files only to the WORDFILE directory, the command is:

**RESTORE A: C:\WORDFILE\ \*.LET/P**

After keying-in the command, you are prompted to insert the disks until the files are found.

**Self-check Activity**

RESTORE the .LTR files to the WORDFILE directory.

**Solution**

**RESTORE A: C:\WORDFILE\\*.LTR/P**

**XCOPY**

XCOPY was introduced in Version 3.2 of MS-DOS and is a combination of the most useful features of COPY and BACKUP. It is, in fact, a good example of having the best of both worlds, so, if you have this utility, use it in place of BACKUP. When used with the /M option XCOPY is much superior to and faster than BACKUP, and, like COPY, it produces usable files (that is, there is no need to use RESTORE), and places them contiguously on the destination disk. When the destination disk runs out of space, you simply insert a replacement disk and re-enter the command. Because of the presence of /M, the copied files will not be recopied.

The form of the command is:

**XCOPY s:[\path][filename] [t:][\path][filename][option][option]...**
or
**XCOPY [s:]\path[filename] [t:][\path][filename][option][option]...**
or
**XCOPY [s:][\path]filename [t:][\path][filename][option][option]...**

**Note:** At least one of the following must be included in the command: source drive, path, or filename (wildcards can be used). If the named destination directory does not exist, XCOPY will create it.

XCOPY command options:

| | |
|---|---|
| /A | copy files only if archive attribute is set to on. **Note:** Archive attribute remains set after copying, but see /M (refer to section above on BACKUP for explanation of archive attribute) |
| /D:dd-mm-yy | copy files which have been changed on or after date indicated |
| /E | copy all subdirectories, even if empty (used only in conjunction with /S) |
| /M | copy files only if archive attribute is set to on. **Note:** Archive attribute is set to off after copying |
| /P | prompt for permission to restore hidden or read-only files |
| /S | copy files in current directory and its subdirectories (creates directory structure on destination disk if they do not already exist) |
| /V | verify files as they are copied to ensure that they do not differ from original |
| /W | wait until a key is pressed before copying (allowing replacement of disks). |

One drawback of XCOPY is that it cannot cope with a very large file; for that you must resort to BACKUP. However, to repeat advice already given, where documents are going to be lengthy, create them as a series of small files and chain them at print out time. That way, you will always be able to call on XCOPY.

Examples of XCOPY commands are:

**XCOPY C:\WORDFILE\\*.\* A:/M**

which copies to disk A only those files in the WORDFILE directory which have been modified or created since previous backup, and sets the archive attribute to off, and:

**XCOPY C:\DATAFILE\\*.INV A:/D:31–12–90**

which copies to disk A only those files in the DATAFILE directory with the .INV extension which were created on or after 31 December 1990.

**Self-check Activity**

What XCOPY command is required to (i) back-up all files on drive C, whose filenames begin with DATE, (ii) back-up the same files but pause for a key to be pressed before each file is copied?

**Solution**

(i)   **XCOPY C:\DATE*.* A:/S**

(ii)  **XCOPY C:\DATE*.* A:/S/W**

Chapter 8 discusses operational policies for effecting efficient backup systems, but it is clear from this chapter that MS-DOS provides backup tools which suit most occasions. The range of options in executing backups allows us to create ways of dealing with data security which take much of the effort out of what can be an inconvenient chore. However, a moment's thought about the consequences of a major data loss should motivate even the most reluctant among us to set up a system to safeguard against such an event. It is quite a straightforward task, and in Chapter 9 instructions are given on how to make it even less onerous by combining a range of backup commands into utility programs.

**EXERCISES**

7.1  Which backup command is appropriate for the following types of files: (i) applications software packages, (ii) a boilerplate for a letter to notify customers of discount bargains, (iii) updated customer orders, (iv) an enquiry for information about a new product, (v) system software, (vi) chapters in a book?

7.2  What form would the BACKUP command take if you wish to back-up only those letters (extension .LET) created or changed since the previous backup?

7.3  What adverse effect would the following have if it were the regular BACKUP command, and what is required to rectify it?

    **BACKUP C: A:/S/M**

7.4  What is the BACKUP command, and the equivalent XCOPY command, to take backups of files with the extension .DOC which were modified since the previous backup?

7.5  Assuming you are in the Root Directory of a hard disk, what is the COPY command required to back-up all files with the .LET extension from the LETTERS directory to a floppy disk in drive A?

7.6  Go into the INVOICES directory, and create two new files with the extension .INV, then back-up these files to a clean, formatted backup disk.

# 8 Securing Data

## INTRODUCTION

Occasionally you see newspaper reports about computer frauds on a grand scale, or about deliberate destruction of computer data in corporate organisations, or stories about operator or programmer errors resulting in people receiving demands for payment of enormous sums of money for goods or services they neither received nor ordered. Although such occurrences are very rare, they do serve to remind us that things can go very wrong with computers and that preventative measures must be taken to secure data.

Large financial institutions in the City of London take what may seem like extreme precautions. It is known that at least one organisation ferries its backups daily to a location outside London adjacent to a motorway, and in the event of a breakdown of their own computer, particularly if the building in which it is housed is severely damaged, immediate access to a replacement mainframe computer for a period of one month has been contracted. The building where the backups are stored will be used to house a new computer if damage to their headquarters cannot be repaired within a month. The cost involved is enormous, but it does give some idea of not only how valuable data is to a business, but also how information technology, in spite of its reliability, makes us very vulnerable to its failures.

Although your personal computer may appear small beer beside huge systems which attract wide publicity when things go wrong, the data it generates is an extremely valuable resource for the business or enterprise in which you are involved. It is therefore essential that it is adequately protected against interference or corruption for whatever reason.

Furthermore, you are obliged to comply with the requirements of the Data Protection Act which regulates the use of computerised data held on individuals and insists that the data registered under its terms is secured. In other words, data must be kept up to date and accurate, and must be available only to authorised persons.

The office or building in which your computer is housed may well be vulnerable to breaches of data security and contraventions of the Data Protection Act. While the same degree of risk to data integrity does not apply if you are working from home, it would be imprudent to assume that there is no possibility of your data being harmed or the Data Protection Act being infringed. So, regardless of your working location, steps should be taken to safeguard the system in general, and the integrity of your data in particular.

**RISKS TO DATA**

To be more specific, the risks to data include:
- loss;
- accidental corruption;
- deliberate corruption;
- theft;
- unauthorised disclosure.

Human error is probably the major cause of data loss and accidental corruption. Prevention is the best solution to this problem. First, by enhancing your skills in using your personal computer, you reduce the possibilities of errors occurring, and second, by establishing a systematic backup system you can ensure that all important data is duplicated. Although Chapter 7 describes the techniques of backup procedures, it does not advocate any particular plan, other than a daily backup using COPY, BACKUP or XCOPY at the end of the working day, but you would be well advised to use a more defensive approach. In other words, assume that something will go wrong.

**ORGANISING FOR BACKUPS**

While the importance of backing-up has been rightly emphasised, it is possible to be overzealous. For example, if you write letters in reply to casual enquiries about the cost of your latest range in dried flowers, is there any point in keeping a copy? Perhaps, if you wanted to contact the enquirers later to encourage them to place orders, otherwise backing-up these types of letters serves no purpose. In addition, you should remove them from your working disks to prevent clutter. But how should you go about backing-up important data? It depends on the nature of the documents concerned. There are, for example, documents which, once completed, are not subject to change, and therefore are best archived. They include letters, reports, statements, etc. On the other hand, documents which are subject to constant updating, such as customer orders, should have backups which are also constantly renewed. Each type of document is dealt with in turn.

**Archiving**

Backing-up the one-off document is quite straightforward. If you are selective in what you regard as important, then COPY will probably serve your needs quite well. It is likely that the copy facility in the applications software is adequate for this kind of backup. If your work is a long document which requires a lengthy period of preparation, COPY is also the appropriate backup command (remember to break the long document into smaller modules). A report or book would fall into this category. As you work on it, copies are maintained on the working disk, as well as on a backup disk. But when you have finished the document, it should be removed from the working disk, and kept on the backup archives. But to be on the safe side, make copies of the archived disks.

Small documents, particularly those such as letters, which are written in one sitting, should be archived upon completion. If you keep printed copies of these as well, you should ask yourself if there is any need to keep both forms of backup. Whether you use COPY, BACKUP or XCOPY for archiving depends on the number of such documents processed daily. If you adopt a selective approach, then COPY serves you best, otherwise BACKUP or XCOPY is more appropriate.

Boilerplates should always be backed-up, and any which are used regularly should be maintained on the working disk also. COPY is the appropriate command, and you should reserve a backup disk specifically for them. In fact, it is advisable to adopt this as a general principle when using COPY or XCOPY, and organise backup disks in categories which reflect the type of data on them. It is equally important to label the disks clearly to show content and date of backup. And, if you use BACKUP, remember to indicate sequence as well; it will save time if you have to use RESTORE.

### Cyclic Backing-Up

A different approach is adopted for data which is constantly updated. What is needed here is a system which cycles backups. For example, if you supply shops with perishable goods which have a quick turnover, and your customers place orders whenever their stock need replenishing you will generate a large number of transactions each day so a set of backup disks is used as indicated in Figure 8.1. This is known as the *three-generation* system, and works as follows. When processing for the day is complete, a disk (disk 1), known as the *son*, is used for backup. On the following day this disk takes on the status of *father*, and a second backup disk (disk 2) becomes the *son*. Next day, disk 1 becomes a *grandfather*, disk 2 becomes *father*, and disk 3 is the *son*. Then on the fourth day, disk 1 becomes the *son* again, so the data backed-up on to it three days earlier is erased and new data is recorded in its place.

|           | disk |
|-----------|------|
| Monday    | 1    |
| Tuesday   | 2    |
| Wednesday | 3    |
| Thursday  | 1    |
| Friday    | 2    |
| Monday    | 3    |

**Figure 8.1    The Three-Generation Backup System**

The advantage of this system is that when data files are corrupted or lost, the situation can be quickly retrieved. For example, if an error occurs during Wednesday, you can copy the files saved on Tuesday back on to your working disk, then enter Wednesday's data again from the keyboard. In other words, only one day's work at most is lost. The backup cycle could take place twice each day, thus ensuring that no more than a half-day's work is lost at any one time, but it is necessary to use more than three disks in these circumstances, possibly as many as six. The three-generations system provides a high degree of security against accidental data loss or corruption, and should be implemented in systems which are constantly modifying files.

## DELIBERATE CORRUPTION, THEFT AND UNAUTHORISED DISCLOSURE

Preventing deliberate corruption, theft and unauthorised disclosure of data is difficult when your personal computer is not dedicated to a specific task, such as processing accounts. In these circumstances you can establish a limited access system by isolating the machine, both physically and operationally, and thus deny access to unauthorised users. On the other hand, when it is a general office tool, access to the computer is often too readily available because it is frequently installed in an area where many people come and go. Nevertheless, you should make every attempt to safeguard your system by considering the following guidelines and taking on board those which afford adequate protection.

**Physical Security**

• *Allow access to the personal computer to authorised personnel only.* This may seem to be irrelevant to users in very small businesses where there may be no more than a few people, but where there are staff who have no need to use the computer, it should be made clear that they must not touch it. In a manual system, if their duties do not require them to extract information directly from customer files, for example, they would not be allowed access to those files. So think of the computer system in a similar way.

Of course, you may be anxious to give others in the business experience in computer usage. If so, access to a machine which holds data essential to the business should take place only under the supervision of someone who can be relied upon to safeguard the system.

•*Do not position a personal computer so that the screen can be viewed by unauthorised individuals.* It is not at all unusual to see computers set up so that the screen is fully visible to anyone in the general vicinity, including areas where outsiders are accommodated while waiting to see staff members. If business transaction data is revealed in this way, clients and customers are likely to take exception to its public display. Furthermore, if the data is of a personal nature, the Data Protection Act is being contravened. Many factors must be accommodated when positioning a computer, for example ergonomic factors concerned with reducing user strain, but privacy of data display is not an optional extra.

•*When unattended, the personal computer should be in a room which is locked.* This recommendation may be impossible to put into practice in a small business which has no more than one or two rooms. But it is possible to lock computers, so where this sort of security is available, it should be used fastidiously. Should locking the machine not be an option, software 'locks' can be implemented, for example, keying-in a password to gain access to applications or system programs. Some information is provided about this type of system in the section on Software Security below, but it is seldom as effective as a physical lock.

•*Never leave personal data applications running when the personal computer is unattended.* Again, it is surprising how often computers are left unattended for long periods with programs running, particularly where visitors are accommodated. A child attracted to the colourful 'toy' on the desk top could wipe out masses of data by accident. An inexperienced user, with a sudden urge to exercise newly developed skills, could clean off all the data on a hard disk by the simple FORMAT command. So think of the harm a malicious, competent user could inflict. Regardless of the size of the business, there is only one rule: close down the system when it is not attended by an authorised user.

•*Computer storage media, including backups, should be locked away when not in use.* First of all, all original applications and systems disks and their non-working backups, and data backups, should be locked away permanently, and they should be stored well away from the computer. Working copies of programs and data should likewise be locked away when not in use. The possibility of damage caused by fire should be considered in deciding locations for storage: the position of the storage unit, and the material of its construction, etc. Keeping the storage location well away from the computer is based on the reasonable assumption that, unless the area concerned is completely destroyed, then there is a high possibility that one or other will not suffer damage. Opportunities for theft are also reduced when this storage system is used, so even if you are unfortunate enough to lose your hardware, your important data is likely to escape notice.

It is well worth considering storing copies of applications software away from the building in which the business is housed. They can be taken home, for example, and left there until needed again. Treating cyclic data backups in the same way is not so convenient because, unless you are willing to do so, you will need someone else to carry them back and forward each day. However, as a minimum precaution, you should store working disks and backup disks in different locations within the business. The more widely spaced they are, the less are the chances of complete loss. Equally, if you produce more than one set of backups, select a separate storage place for the additional set(s). Inconvenient, you may think, but there is little point in establishing a reliable backup system which is negated by a careless approach to storage.

## Software Security

Software security generally involves entering a password before the system allows access. This is a very convenient and cheap way to safeguard your system. Although password-only access can be set up by modifying certain MS-DOS files, particularly AUTOEXEC.BAT and COMMAND.COM, the inconvenience involved makes buying a software utility specifically designed for the job a more appropriate alternative by far. It is also a more secure method. Some applications software packages also have built-in password utilities, so you should use these facilities if available.

Should you adopt this approach, it is necessary to change passwords frequently. And choose words or groups of characters which would not easily be guessed (for example, avoid your name, your spouse's name, or Jaguar, if you own one). Furthermore, the passwords should be disclosed to authorised users only. Finally, passwords should not be noted on pieces of paper and pinned to boards, or left in drawers or on desk tops. It is better that they are not written at all, but if memorising a password is a problem, then, when written, it should be stored in a way which does not identify it.

Encrypting files, that is, converting them into code, is another method of software security. Utility software can be obtained for this purpose, and it does guard against casual, unauthorised, prying eyes. However, like all software locking systems, it should be used in conjunction with, not as a replacement for, physical security.

## Operational Security

Operational security refers to a system which denies unauthorised persons access to instructional material describing the operation of an application, for example, a database, and which prevents them from being able to examine specifications which describe the content and structure of files in an application. This information should be locked away when not in use.

Printouts of data should also be locked away. There is little point in securing data stored on magnetic media, and then making no attempt to protect hard copies. Equally, printouts which are no longer required should be destroyed, and if outside contractors are involved, the printouts should not be left for collection in an area which is open to the public, particularly if the files contain personal information.

Establishing a security system to protect data should also take account of the damage which can be inflicted on equipment through generally careless habits in the vicinity of the computer. For example, liquid spilled on a keyboard could put the system out of action, and crumbs could be equally damaging, so, to ensure no such failures occur, coffee breaks should be taken well away from the computer.

Particles of smoke can affect the efficiency of disk operation by lodging between the disk surface and the recording head, corrupting data as a result. Floppy disks can be damaged by the pressure of weight; by exposure to heat or to strong magnetic fields; by contact with greasy fingers; and through general rough treatment. So, examples of the type of treatment which could impair them are: using them as coffee-cup coasters; leaving them close to a radiator or on top of the monitor; touching the recording surfaces; and putting them into the drive without due attention.

## DATA PROTECTION ACT

The Data Protection Act (1984) was introduced in response to fears that data held or processed on computers might be misused. It regulates the use of computerised information about living, identifiable individuals, and requires that all such data be registered with the Data Protection Registrar, and used only in accordance with the terms under which it is registered. Registered data must be held securely, must be accurate and must not be disclosed to unauthorised persons. Furthermore, individuals have the right of access to information held about them.

The Act reinforces the need for data security, so by following the general guidelines advocated in this chapter, you will go a long way towards ensuring that you do not fall foul of its terms.

# Part III

This part introduces more advanced features of MS-DOS, but maintains the practical approach adopted in earlier parts. The focus is on batch files.

**Chapter 9: Batch Files**

This chapter focuses on one topic, namely the creation and application of *batch* files. It starts by showing simple batch file programs which execute single MS-DOS commands. The use of ECHO is explained and advice on correcting errors is given. Batch files with more than one command are then described, and the use of EDLIN and RPED is discussed in relation to their preparation. Finally, examples show how to design single batch files which can be used as comprehensive backup programs.

**Chapter 10: Interfaces**

This chapter is concerned with setting up a system interface which is activated at boot-up; this is achieved by setting up a path in the AUTOEXEC.BAT file to gain access to the full range of MS-DOS external commands, and by providing a set of batch files which can be used to start applications and systems programs. In addition, instructions are given on how to construct a safe FORMAT routine, and the CONFIG.SYS file is examined, and an explanation of its function presented.

# 9 Batch Files

**INTRODUCTION**

For many of the activities and exercises in this chapter, it is assumed that certain files exist as the result of work carried out in previous chapters. If you have lost them along the way, it will be necessary to create new files to replace the missing ones as required.

In Chapters 6 and 7 you used MS-DOS commands one at a time; that is, each command was executed before you keyed-in another. However, there is a very convenient alternative. Commands can be stored in one file, then on activating the file, MS-DOS executes the commands in sequence. This type of file is known as a *batch* file because it causes MS-DOS to process a batch of commands.

Batch files are characterised by the extension .BAT, and in Chapter 6 it was pointed out that .BAT indicates a command file. What is particularly interesting about batch files is that they give us a simple way of exercising a great deal of control over the operating system. All batch files are run in the same way as MS-DOS commands, that is the filename is keyed-in after the prompt. For example a batch file with the filename CLEAR.BAT is executed by typing-in **CLEAR** at the MS-DOS prompt and pressing <Return>.

Although you may feel that there is really no need to get so involved with a computer when all you want to do is run applications software, you will find that batch file programs simplify the use of file management. You will also find that this degree of control requires the acquisition of few new skills because, for the most part, you use the commands which you learned in Chapters 4, 6 and 7. However, once you have mastered these basic programs, you can independently progress to writing many more of your own batch files.

### Organising a Disk for Batch Files

If you have a hard disk, it is best to keep all batch files in one directory created for them. So go ahead now and create a new directory in the Root Directory and name it BATCH, and change to this new directory with CD\BATCH.

If you do not have a hard disk, you should keep all batch files on a single floppy. Furthermore, you should format the disk using the /S option, as shown in Chapter 6, so that it can be used to boot-up your computer. Having done this, COMMAND.COM and the hidden systems files are on the disk, so all the MS-DOS internal commands are available to you on the BATCH disk.

### BATCH FILES WITH SINGLE COMMANDS

The first batch file we create is purely for the purpose of illustration and uses the internal command DIR. So key-in **COPY CON FIRST.BAT**, then, on the following line key-in the contents of the batch file, namely:

### DIR

Do not forget to finish off by going to a new line and entering <**F6**>, after which you key-in the batch file command:

### FIRST

and a directory listing, preceded by **DIR**, appears on screen. It would, of course, be much more sensible to use DIR rather than FIRST, but the example shows how a batch file works.

### Self-check Activity

Using COPY CON write and execute a batch file, DISPLAY.BAT, which displays the contents of FIRST.BAT on screen.

### Solution

Start off by keying-in **COPY CON DISPLAY.BAT**, followed on the next line by the contents of the file, namely:

### TYPE FIRST.BAT

Do not forget to finish off with <**F6**>, then key-in **FIRST**, after which you should see:

**TYPE FIRST.BAT**
**DIR**

### The ECHO Command

The reason for the appearance of DIR on the first line of the screen display when FIRST executes, and TYPE FIRST.BAT when DISPLAY executes, is that instructions in batch files are echoed on the screen, followed by the output of the instructions. To prevent this happening, a special batch file command is used, namely ECHO. ECHO, an internal command, is either ON or OFF, the default being ON, so you simply include ECHO OFF as the first line in the batch file as follows:

**ECHO OFF**
**DIR**

Write this version of the batch file, using COPY CON as before. On this occasion the screen output begins with **ECHO OFF**, followed by the listing. This may seem no better than the **DIR** command appearing on the screen, but if there were three or more instructions in the file, only **ECHO OFF** appears in the output. However, you can get rid of this line as well by using the CLS internal command which clears the screen and returns the cursor to the top left. Try writing FIRST.BAT as:

**ECHO OFF**
**CLS**
**DIR**

What happens is that, although **ECHO OFF** appears, it does so only for a fleeting moment, before CLS removes it from the screen. Another reason to use CLS is that it gets rid of all other output, leaving you with a clear screen, except for the program output, so it is good practice to start off all batch files with ECHO OFF and CLS.

If you have MS-DOS 3.3 or later, there is another way to achieve the same objective, namely, put the @ sign immediately in front of ECHO OFF. This has the effect of suppressing the screen appearance of ECHO OFF altogether:

**@ECHO OFF**
**CLS**

**Note:** In spite of its virtues, it is better not to insert ECHO OFF until after the program executes successfully. By following this advice, mistakes you may make in writing the file are easier to trace and correct. This is because both the error messages, and the commands they are associated with, are displayed on the screen when you execute the batch file command. By including ECHO OFF you see the error messages only, hence it is advisable to omit it initially. (Further information is provided in a later section on Errors in Batch Files.)

### Self-check Activity

Using COPY CON, write a batch file, WIPEOUT.BAT, which deletes DISPLAY.BAT.

### Solution

**ECHO OFF**
**CLS**
**DEL DISPLAY.BAT**

### The PRINT Command

So far, only internal commands have been used in our batch files. Now you can try the external MS-DOS command, PRINT. But first copy PRINT.COM (or PRINT.EXE if that is the version you have) into your BATCH directory on the hard disk, or on to your BATCH floppy. When you have done this, rewrite DISPLAY.BAT (not forgetting the advice about ECHO OFF) as:

**ECHO OFF**

**CLS**

**PRINT WIPEOUT.BAT**

When DISPLAY is executed, **Name of list device [PRN]:** appears on screen. You need only to press return in response. Two other messages then appear on screen:

**Resident part of PRINT installed**

**C:\BATCH\WIPEOUT.BAT is currently being printed**

and at the same time, the contents of WIPEOUT.BAT are printed.

(The floppy version displays **A:WIPEOUT.BAT** instead of the hard disk directory path.)

**Self-check Activity**

Write and execute a batch file which prints FIRST.BAT

**Solution**

> **ECHO OFF**
> **CLS**
> **PRINT FIRST.BAT**

## BATCH FILES WITH A SEQUENCE OF COMMANDS

Quite clearly, there is little difficulty in writing very simple, single command batch files. Furthermore, as was pointed out, there is seldom any need to use batch files in this way. So we now proceed to creating files containing a sequence of commands, and you will find that batch files do have a very valuable contribution to make to file maintenance.

The first example uses the CD and DIR commands to list files in the WORDFILE directory. Assuming you are in the BATCH directory of your hard disk, four steps are required to create the batch file, which we name EX1DIR.BAT:

(i)   Clear the screen, using **CLS**

(ii)  Change to the WORDFILE directory, using **CD\WORDFILE**

(iii) List the directory files, using **DIR**

(iv)  Return to the BATCH directory, using **CD\BATCH**

Hence the batch file consists of four lines as follows:

> **CLS**
> **CD\UWORDFILE**
> **DIR**
> **CD\UBATCH**

Upon successful execution, you see a directory listing of WORDFILE on the screen, followed by the MS-DOS prompt. (At this stage, insert

ECHO OFF on the first line of EX1DIR.BAT.)

If you have a twin floppy disk machine, create EX1DIR.BAT on your BATCH disk. It will differ somewhat from the hard disk version of EX1DIR.BAT, because, instead of changing directories only, you change to a different disk, namely the disk which contains the appropriate directories. This disk is placed in drive B. The steps required are:

(i)    Clear the screen, using **CLS**

(ii)   Change the current drive from A to B, using **B:**

(iii)  Change to the WORDFILE directory, using **CD\WORDFILE**

(iv)   List the directory files, using **DIR**

(v)    Return to drive A, using **A:**

Hence the batch file consists of five lines as follows:

**CLS**
**B:**
**CD\UWORDFILE**
**DIR**
**A:**

### Self-check Activity

(For this activity make sure that MYNAME.DOC is in the WORDS directory. If not, create the file with your name as the contents.)

Write and execute a batch file, SHOWNAME.BAT, which (i) goes to the WORDS directory, (ii) displays the contents of MYNAME.DOC on screen, (iii) returns to the BATCH directory (or disk).

### Solution

| *(hard disk)* | *(twin floppy disks)* |
|---|---|
| **ECHO OFF** | **ECHO OFF** |
| **CLS** | **CLS** |
| **CD\WORDS** | **B:** |
| **TYPE MYNAME.DOC** | **CD\WORDS** |
| **CD\BATCH** | **TYPE MYNAME.DOC** |
|  | **A:** |

## Errors in Batch Files

What happens when errors occur in batch files? Fortunately, MS-DOS is quite good at letting us know both where the error lies and what is causing it. Let us assume that you made an error in EX1DIR.BAT, typing DIP instead of DIR/P. When you run the program, the screen display will show:

**C:\>CD\WORDFILE**
**C:\WORDFILE>DIP**
**Bad command or file name**

**C:\<\BATCH**

**C:\**

The location and cause of the error are identified in a screen message, namely that DIP is a 'bad command'. You can see how useful this information is, enabling you to quickly correct the single error. Had you included ECHO OFF, the error message would be displayed, but not the command which caused it, and you might have wasted considerable time making many failed attempts to correct before being successful. Obviously, the longer your batch file, the greater the need to be able to see the cause of errors.

Another feature of this display is that it illustrates the operation of a batch file. You can see how the file continues to activate the command on each line before finishing. Furthermore, you can see that the error within the batch file does not stop the execution of the batch file itself.

### Self-check Activity

Assuming that you are in the BATCH directory (or BATCH disk), what output results when EX1DIR executes if there is a spelling mistake in WORDFILE. (Try to figure it out before you run it.)

| *(hard disk)* | *(twin floppy disks)* |
|---|---|
| **ECHO OFF** | **ECHO OFF** |
| **CLS** | **CLS** |
| **CD\WORRFILE** | **B:** |
| **DIR** | **CD\WORRFILE** |
| **CD\BATCH** | **DIR** |
| | **A:** |

**Solution**

The error message, **Invalid directory**, appears after the **CD\WORRFILE** command line is echoed, then the BATCH directory (or Root Directory on the B drive) is listed. In other words, there is no directory change to WORDFILE.

### EDITORS FOR WRITING AND MODIFYING FILES

So far, you have been told to use COPY CON to prepare files, mainly because it is easy to use, it is suitable for very short files, and it is an internal MS-DOS command. Unfortunately this method has severe limitations as you cannot make changes to a file prepared by COPY CON; it is only possible to rewrite the entire file. There are, however, alternatives in MS-DOS, the best known, but least appealing, being an editing system called EDLIN (EDLIN.COM or EDLIN.EXE). Amstrad owners are fortunate to have the RPED editor as well (RPED.EXE). It is the easier of the two to use by a long way, and although it has limitations, it is appropriate for all the editing you are asked to do in this book. Full instructions for using both EDLIN and RPED are in your computer manual, but to use either, key-in:

**EDLIN filename**

or

**RPED filename**

Note: The filename must include the extension.

Another editor, which you may find more user-friendly than EDLIN is your word processor. But, be sure that you use it in *non-document* mode. All word processors provide the choice of *document* or *non-document* mode. For all general word processing purposes, you use the former. Non-document mode is more like using a typewriter where you have to press the <Return> at the end of lines, and so on, and is used for writing programs (such as batch files).

If you wish to use your word processor to create .BAT files, it is first of all necessary to change to the word processor directory to write the files, then copy them to the BATCH directory. You then return to the BATCH directory. Subsequent editing requires the same operation. If, however, you decide not to use your word processor, copy EDLIN-.COM (or EDLIN.EXE) to your BATCH directory (or RPED.EXE if you have it). You can then write the files without leaving the BATCH directory. Users of twin floppy machines follow the same procedure, but in relation to a BATCH disk rather than a directory.

## BATCH FILES AS BACKUP ROUTINES

### Using COPY

The examples given so far are in the nature of exercises to demonstrate the use of batch files. Now we look at the type of batch files which are of direct practical value to you. For example, a useful way to carry out a daily backup routine for .BAT files, which also purges .BAK files, is to create a batch file to do the job. This could be written for any directory but, for the sake of illustration, we use the BATCH directory batch files. Before you carry out this activity, create two files with the .BAK extension in BATCH for the sake of the exercise. Then write the following file, BACKEX1.BAT. (**Note:** Do not name it BACKUP-.BAT, as the MS-DOS BACKUP command will be activated instead.)

```
ECHO OFF
CLS
CD\BATCH
COPY *.BAT A:
DEL *.BAK
DIR
```

This batch file copies all .BAT files, deletes all .BAK files, then lists the BATCH directory.

For floppy disk users, backing up from drive A to B using COPY, the file is as follows:

```
ECHO OFF
CLS
COPY *.BAT B:
DEL *.BAK
DIR
```

You should now find no difficulty in creating a batch file to back-up the .BAT files, and purge the .BAK files in several directories, for example, in WORDFILE, WORDS, DATAFILE and DATABASE. Before doing so, to let us check the outcome of executing the batch file, create two .BAT files and two .BAK files in each of the four directories. Next write the file, BACKALL1.BAT, as follows:

```
ECHO OFF
CLS
CD\WORDFILE
COPY *.BAT A:
DEL *.BAK
CD\WORDS
COPY *.BAT A:
DEL *.BAK
CD\DATAFILE
COPY *.BAT A:
DEL *.BAK
CD\DATABASE
COPY *.BAT A:
DEL *.BAK
CD\BATCH
```

### Self-check Activity

What changes are necessary in BACKALL1.BAK so that all files in the directories are backed up?

### Solution

The COPY command lines are changed to **COPY *.* A:** in each case.

### Using BACKUP

Generally BACKUP is a more refined and precise tool when regular backing-up of large amounts of data is required, but you must exercise care because it cannot be used in a blanket fashion as can COPY. It was pointed out in Chapter 7 that if the option /A is not used, BACKUP deletes the target disk before writing to it. While this is immaterial on the first backup, it obviously would be disastrous for subsequent backups. Yet the /A option stops copying taking place unless BACKUP has previously put files on the target disk. This means that the first backup must take place without the /A option, thereafter it should be included, as in BACKALL2.BAT which follows. (**Note:** For the sake of checking the effects of executing BACKALL2.BAT, do not forget to reinstate the .BAK files deleted by BACKALL1.BAT.)

```
ECHO OFF
CLS
```

```
CD\WORDFILE
BACKUP *.BAT A:/M/A
DEL *.BAK
CD\WORDS
BACKUP *.BAT A:/M/A
DEL *.BAK
CD\DATAFILE
BACKUP *.BAT A:/M/A
DEL *.BAK
CD\DATABASE
BACKUP *.BAT A:/M/A
DEL *.BAK
CD\BATCH
```

Each time the BACKUP command is activated, you are given an opportunity to insert a different disk. This is very convenient and allows you to reserve a separate backup disk for each directory.

### Self-check Activity

If a batch file were written to carry out the initial backup, how would it differ from BACKALL2.BAT?

### Solution

The /A option would be omitted.

### Pausing Batch File Execution

It is useful to see directory listings after each purge but this is not possible by simply inserting DIR commands in BACKALL1.BAT and BACKALL2.BAT because the listings, before they could be examined, would be removed from the screen by the action of the subsequent commands. There is, however, an internal command (PAUSE) which causes the execution of a batch file to be delayed until a key is pressed. During the pause, the message **Strike any key when ready** is displayed. Using PAUSE, the batch file (name it BACKALL3.BAT) becomes:

```
ECHO OFF
CLS
CD\WORDFILE
BACKUP *.BAT A:/M/A
DEL *.BAK
```

```
DIR
PAUSE
CD\WORDS
BACKUP *.BAT A:/M/A
DEL *.BAK
DIR
PAUSE
CD\DATAFILE
BACKUP *.BAT A:/M/A
DEL *.BAK
DIR
PAUSE
CD\DATABASE
BACKUP *.BAT A:/M/A
DEL *.BAK
DIR
PAUSE
CD\BATCH
```

**Self-check Activity**

Create two .LTR files in WORDFILE and in WORDS, then write and execute a batch file program which backs-up these files before erasing them from the working disk. A listing of each directory is provided after each backup and purge has been completed. Finally, the program takes you to the BATCH directory.

**Solution**

```
ECHO OFF
CLS
CD\WORDFILE
BACKUP *.LTR A:/M/A
DEL *.LTR
DIR
PAUSE
CD\WORDS
BACKUP *.LTR A:/M/A
DEL *.LTR
DIR
PAUSE
CD\BATCH
```

## SUMMARY

This chapter has introduced you to programming using the MS-DOS language. As you can now see, it is not difficult to apply the knowledge gained in earlier chapters, and there is no reason why you should not experiment by creating batch files with MS-DOS commands other than those used here. In the next chapter, you are shown how to use batch files as a means of creating a friendly interface between MS-DOS and your applications program. This is achieved by taking advantage of one of the most useful of all files in MS-DOS, namely, AUTOEXEC.BAT, particularly in relation to the PATH command which allows you to configure your personal computer so that directory changing becomes almost unnecessary.

## EXERCISES

9.1  Write and execute a single command batch file, NEWPRMPT.BAT which changes your prompt to **Enter data here**.

9.2  What is the screen output for the following batch program, TYPENAME.BAT, which has two spelling mistakes: in the command TYPE, and in the directory name BATCH?

```
ECHO OFF
CLS
CD\WORDS
TPYE MYNAME.DOC
CD\BATCH
DIR
```

9.3  Write and execute a batch file, PRNTNAME.BAT, which prints out your name from MYNAME.DOC in WORDS, then displays a listing of the Root Directory on your hard disk.

Twin floppy disk users: place the BATCH disk in drive A, and the disk with WORDS in drive B. Display the Root Directory listing from drive B.

9.4  Create two files in the WORDFILE directory, FRIEND1.DOC and FRIEND2.DOC, entering the name of a different friend in each. Then, going to your BATCH directory, write and execute a batch file, FRIENDS.BAT, which displays the two names on screen, but which waits for you to press a key before the second name appears.

Twin floppy disk users: place the BATCH disk in drive A, and the disk with WORDFILE in drive B.

9.5 Write and execute a batch file which copies FRIEND1.DOC and FRIEND2.DOC to WORDS, then deletes the original files from WORDFILE.

Twin floppy disk users: follow the directions given in 9.4.

9.6 Write and execute a batch file, NEWDIR.BAT, in the BATCH directory, or disk, which (i) creates the directory, NEW, in the Root Directory, (ii) copies FRIEND1.DOC from WORDS to NEW, (iii) displays the contents of FRIEND1.DOC on screen.

Twin floppy disk users: place the BATCH disk in drive A, and the disk with WORDS in drive B. Create NEW on disk B.

(**Tip:** If you manage to create the NEW directory, but make other errors in NEWDIR.BAT, it will be necessary to delete NEW before NEWDIR.BAT runs successfully on subsequent tries. See Chapter 6 for information on deleting directories.)

# 10 Interfaces

## INTRODUCTION

It has been pointed out that the Root Directory on a hard disk should not be cluttered. However, it is only in this chapter that you find out how to organise your directory system to avoid clutter, the reason being that it is better that you cover the material in most of the earlier chapters before taking on the task of organising files on your hard disk.

Equally, if your machine has twin floppy disks, your boot-up disk should not be full of unwanted files, and your other disks should be organised in much the same way as the directory system on a hard disk. In fact, floppy disks probably lend themselves to more disciplined organisation because users are always conscious of the limitations imposed by the amount of data or programs they can hold. But, in general, if those of you with floppy drives only equate disks with directories, most of the advice in this chapter will be of direct relevance.

What you learn in this chapter is (i) which MS-DOS files to place in the Root Directory, (ii) how to organise the rest of the MS-DOS files, and (iii) how to configure (set up) your personal computer system to activate any program file even if it is not in the current directory; in other words how to create a friendly computer interface.

Before going any further, make sure that you have backups of all your system and applications software. If you have the original masters only, remember the advice in Chapter 7 about backing-up with DISKCOPY. In addition, if you have not already done so, take backups of all data files which you need. The first principle to apply, without exception, is always back-up before undertaking any housekeeping jobs on your computer.

**Note:** To find out what directories and subdirectories are on a hard disk, use the MS-DOS external command TREE. It may be necessary to copy TREE.COM (or TREE.EXE) into the Root Directory first. After that, key-in TREE from the Root Directory. To stop the list scrolling, press <Ctrl>-S.

## THE ROOT DIRECTORY FILES

As was indicated in Chapter 4, the only files which are really required in the Root Directory are COMMAND.COM, AUTOEXEC.BAT and CONFIG.SYS and the hidden system files. Nevertheless, several other files which contribute to system configuration should be placed there for convenience. MS-DOS provides facilities to let you configure the computer to fit your own needs, and it is exactly this which you are shown in this chapter.

Start by booting-up your computer, then enter the Root Directory and list its contents on screen. What is displayed depends on a lot of factors, including the way your system software was installed and the version of MS-DOS you have. The next stage is to get the directory system organised so that only a very small number of MS-DOS external command files, and applications programs (and any stray text files which might have landed there) are in the Root Directory.

You have already prepared a directory system for a word processor and a database (WORDS and DATABASE) so there is no reason why these should not be used as appropriate (remembering, however, that WordStar 1512 creates its own directory system which is better not disturbed). If, however, you already have directories for applications software, leave them as they are and delete WORDS and other superfluous directories. Do not forget that, to delete a directory, all files in the directory must first be erased. The next step is to create a directory (in the Root Directory) for MS-DOS external files. For convenience, call the directory DOS, although it is useful to indicate the version in the directory name, for example DOS33 for Version 3.3.

Next get a printout of your Root Directory listing by keying-in:

**DIR > PRN**

This leaves you with a list which enables you to keep track of all the listed files. Start off by identifying those files which are to remain in the Root Directory. These may not be exactly the same as those you have, but many will be. (**Note:** As a general principle, files with the .SYS extension should be in the Root Directory.)

**COMMAND.COM**
**AUTOEXEC.BAT**
**CONFIG.SYS**
**ANSI.SYS**
**COUNTRY.SYS**
**DISPLAY.SYS**
**PRINTER.SYS**
**VDRIVE.SYS**     (or **RAMDRIVE.SYS**)
**KEYBUK.COM**     (or **KEYB.COM**)
**EDLIN.COM**     (or **RPED.EXE**)
**MOUSE.COM**

If there are any applications software files, copy these to appropriate directories, creating new directories where necessary. Next, delete those files in the Root Directory which you have copied.

### Files to Export from the Root Directory

MS-DOS external files can now be copied to the DOS directory. This is just a simple matter of using a wildcard to copy all .EXE and .COM files:

**COPY *.EXE \DOS**

and

**COPY *.COM \DOS**

The one exception is COMMAND.COM, although it is more convenient to copy it with the other .COM files, and then delete it from the DOS directory. Examples of external command files are:

| | |
|---|---|
| **APPEND.EXE** | **GRAPHICS.COM** |
| **ASSIGN.COM** | **JOIN.COM** |
| **ATTRIB.EXE** | **KEYBUK.COM (or KEYB.COM)** |
| **BACKUP.COM** | **LABEL.COM** |
| **CHKDSK.COM** | **MODE.COM** |
| **COMP.COM** | **MORE.COM** |
| **DEBUG.EXE** | **MOUSE.COM** |
| **DISKCOMP.COM** | **PRINT.COM** |
| **DISKCOPY.COM** | **REPLACE.EXE** |
| **EXE2BIN.EXE** | **RESTORE.COM** |
| **EDLIN.COM** | **SORT.COM** |

**FDISK.COM**              **SUBST.EXE**
**FIND.EXE**               **SYS.COM**
**GRAFTABL.COM**           **TREE.COM**
**GRAPHICS.COM**           **XCOPY.COM**

Three of these files are also in the Root Directory list. However, they are used to configure the system, so it is convenient to let them remain in both directories, but you should delete the remaining .COM and .EXE files after copying them to DOS.

There is, however, one external file not included in either list, FORMAT.COM. Because it could be the cause of wiping all the data on your hard disk, it may be advisable to use FORMAT from a floppy. If you wish to have it on the hard disk, however, copy it to DOS. (Later on, advice is given about designing a batch file with a built-in safeguard against accidentally formatting the hard disk.)

You can see from the list of external files that many are not explained in this book. It is, however, more beneficial for you to start by acquiring competence in using a small number of command files selected for the quick return they bring. Your computer manual has full information about the others, and the principles for applying them are exactly the same as for those explained in the book, so you should not hesitate to try them.

Having reorganised the MS-DOS files, the next task you undertake is to configure your computer system. To do this, it is necessary to start by examining the AUTOEXEC.BAT file.

## THE AUTOEXEC.BAT FILE

AUTOEXEC.BAT is a special kind of batch file. When the MS-DOS boot-up routine is activated, it always checks the Root Directory for AUTOEXEC.BAT. On finding it, the computer follows the instructions it finds there. So, by customising AUTOEXEC.BAT, you can exercise great control over the way your personal computer behaves.

### Customising AUTOEXEC.BAT – PROMPT

Customising AUTOEXEC.BAT is explained by showing you (i) how to modify the PROMPT command, and (ii) how to set up directory paths. For the sake of the exercise, the new prompt is:

## MS-DOS RULES THIS COMPUTER

Start by providing yourself with a hard copy of AUTOEXEC.BAT, using PRINT AUTOEXEC.BAT; then you can write your modifications on paper before entering them at the keyboard. (The hard copy also provides a second line of backup defence.)

If you use either EDLIN or RPED for editing, the procedure is as follows:

1 Enter the Root Directory.

2 Edit the AUTOEXEC.BAT file by writing (or rewriting) the PROMPT command as:

### PROMPT MS-DOS RULES THIS COMPUTER

Position the new prompt near the top of the file, but after ECHO OFF and CLS. If these commands are not present, insert them on the first two lines, then enter the PROMPT command on the following line.

3 Save AUTOEXEC.BAT, then reset the computer. (If your computer does not have a reset switch, use <**Ctrl**>-<**Alt**>-<**Del**>; that is, hold <**Ctrl**> and <**Alt**> down simultaneously, then press <**Del**>.)

When the computer reboots, the new MS-DOS prompt appears on the screen. If any problems arise, there is no need to panic, because having saved the original AUTOEXEC.BAT file to another disk you can copy it back to the Root Directory if necessary. However, if there is a difficulty, start all over again and keep trying – the problem will lie in an editing error.

For a prompt which displays the current directory, edit AUTOEXEC.BAT again, and substitute **PROMPT $P$G** for **PROMPT MS-DOS RULES THIS COMPUTER**. If $P$G was in your original prompt, then simply replace AUTOEXEC.BAT with your backup copy. Finally, reset your computer.

### Customising AUTOEXEC.BAT – PATH

At this stage, let us examine the structure of your directories as they now exist. Figure 10.1 illustrates the current position. It is likely that other directories exist on your hard disk; these can be revealed with the

TREE command. WordStar 1512 users, for example, also have the directory structure illustrated in Figure 6.2. If so, with the exception of WordStar 1512, you should consider tidying them up, asking yourself whether you really need all the files saved in them, also asking whether you need all of the directories.

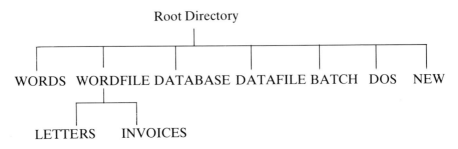

**Figure 10.1    Structure of Directories**

The next task is to create a path in the AUTOEXEC.BAT file which gives access to commands in different directories without leaving the current directory. This is very simply accomplished by using the internal MS-DOS command, PATH. But where should the path take you? You could create a path to take you to every directory, but there is no need to do that. Instead the path has three destinations: the Root Directory, DOS and BATCH. So edit AUTOEXEC.BAT and insert the following line just prior to the PROMPT command line, or add it into the current PATH instruction:

**PATH C:\; C:\DOS; C\:BATCH**

The reason for adding the paths to those already set up, is to maintain access to directories which may be an essential part of your computer's current configuration. When you are fully acquainted with the effects of reorganising paths, you can then, if you wish, make major modifications.

When the PATH has been set, and AUTOEXEC.BAT saved, reboot the computer; after which you are able to activate all the MS-DOS external commands regardless of current directory. But why include the BATCH directory in the path? Because the BATCH directory is the link to the other directories.

## Using Batch Files to Access Applications Programs

To show how batch files can be exploited to provide a means of accessing applications programs, an example rather than an explanation will better facilitate understanding. Assume that you have WordStar in the WORDS directory, and that you wish to activate WordStar with the command WSTAR. You do this by writing a batch file, WSTAR.BAT, which, when executed, goes through the following steps:

Change to WORDS directory, using **CD\WORDS**

Activate WordStar, using **WS**

Return to the BATCH directory, using **CD\BATCH**

List the batch files in the BATCH directory, using **DIR *.BAT**

Hence, the file WSTAR.BAT takes the form:

**ECHO OFF**
**CLS**
**CD\WORDS**
**WS**
**CD\BATCH**
**DIR *.BAT**

The reason for listing the BATCH directory batch files is to provide a *menu* of batch files commands.

As another example, let us assume that you have the relational database VP-Info, and that you have it in the DATABASE directory. VP-Info is started by keying-in VPI, hence the batch file INFO.BAT takes the form:

**ECHO OFF**
**CLS**
**CD\DATABASE**
**VPI**
**CD\BATCH**
**DIR*.BAT**

**Note:** There is no reason why the filenames WS.BAT and VPI.BAT should not be used in preference to WSTAR.BAT and INFO.BAT. Unlike an earlier warning not to call a batch file BACKUP.BAT because BACKUP.COM would respond to the command instead

(.COM files having priority over .BAT files with the same filename), interference would not matter in this case as each pair of programs has the same purpose, that is, the batch files start a process which calls the .COM files into operation.

You can create batch files to start all your applications software. Unfortunately, not all applications software packages allow you to return to BATCH when their execution is finished. The integrated software package, Ability, is an example which leaves you in its own directory. It is possible to prevent this by altering one of Ability's own batch files, but until you are confident enough to tackle this, you can overcome the difficulty by keying-in **CD\BATCH** after you finish with Ability.

Remember also the batch files you created in Chapter 9 activities. Many of these, perhaps modified to suit your system, are useful utilities for backing-up, etc. They should be placed in the BATCH directory (or disk).

**Self-check Activity**

A spreadsheet, started by keying-in **WORKOUT**, is in a directory called SPRSHT. Write a batch file which would activate the spreadsheet, then return you to BATCH and display the batch files on screen.

**Solution**

**ECHO OFF**
**CLS**
**CD\SPRSHT**
**WORKOUT**
**CD\BATCH**
**DIR*.BAT**

**Protection Against Accidentally Formatting the Hard Disk**

So far, the focus has been on the creation of batch files to start applications software. Earlier, the dangers inherent in having FORMAT too readily available were indicated, but by creating a batch file, FORMAT can be rendered safe. To do this, copy FORMAT.COM (or FORMAT.EXE) into the DOS directory if you have not already done so. The next step is to change the name of FORMAT.COM to

XXFORMAT.COM. In doing so, you are ensuring that keying-in FORMAT will not wipe your hard disk. The form of the rename command is:

**REN FORMAT.COM XXFORMAT.COM**

Now write a batch file, FORMAT.BAT as follows:

```
ECHO OFF
CLS
XXFORMAT A:
CD\BATCH
DIR *.BAT
```

Now, when you key-in **FORMAT**, only a floppy disk can be formatted. You might perhaps call this batch file FORMATA.BAT to help you remember that it is for drive A only.

**Self-check Activity**

Write a batch file, FORMATB.BAT, which formats disks in drive B only, then returns to the BATCH directory and displays the .BAT files.

**Solution**

```
ECHO OFF
CLS
XXFORMAT B:
CD\BATCH
DIR *.BAT
```

So far, the only changes made to AUTOEXEC.BAT are concerned with the PROMPT and PATH commands. What about the remainder of AUTOEXEC.BAT? This is best answered by examining one version:

```
ECHO OFF
CLS
PROMPT $P$G
PATH C:\; C:\DOS; C:\BATCH
KEYBUK
MOUSE
CD\BATCH
DIR *.BAT
```

This is a very simple, yet efficient, AUTOEXEC.BAT. The only commands you have not met are KEYBUK and MOUSE. The former is an external command which runs a program to provide the UK keyboard (ensures that UK-type characters are displayed on screen). MOUSE makes the mouse available for input.

## THE CONFIG.SYS FILE

It was recommended earlier that MS-DOS files with the extension .SYS are placed in the Root Directory. These files are called from CONFIG.SYS which sets up certain configuration parameters at boot-up. They are known as device driver files, and are responsible for letting MS-DOS know how to handle input and output from various peripheral hardware devices. There is no need to go into detail about these files, but it is worth letting you examine a typical example of CONFIG.SYS:

**FILES = 20**
**BUFFERS = 10**
**DEVICE = ANSI.SYS**
**DEVICE = VDRIVE.SYS 128**
**COUNTRY = 044**

The implications of this file are as follows. The numbers of files and buffers can be set. FILES = 20 permits up to 20 files to be open at one time; very useful, for example, when using a relational database. A buffer is a block of 528 bytes of memory, so if ten buffers are set, data can be read into memory in 5,280 byte chunks. However, if the program itself uses a very large amount of memory, the number of buffers must be kept small. DEVICE = ANSI.SYS provides enhanced control over the screen and keyboard, while DEVICE = VDRIVE.SYS 128 (RAMDRIVE 128 in the Amstrad PC) sets aside 128K of main memory and treats it as a disk (*virtual* disk or RAM disk). The main advantage is speed of data transfer. COUNTRY = 044 is the configuration for UK use of the computer.

In spite of the recommendation to place .SYS files in the Root Directory, you could put them in DOS with the external files, but, if you do, it is necessary to use paths to set up the device drivers, for example, **DEVICE=\DOS\ANSI.SYS**.

It is unlikely that you need to modify CONFIG.SYS, but if the necessity arises, editing takes place in the usual way. If, for example, you buy an additional hardware peripheral at some time in the future, it might then be necessary to add a new device driver to the CONFIG.SYS file.

Using the BATCH directory and batch files as a means of creating an interface should present you with little difficulty, although getting your disk organised might take some time. Do not try to do it quickly, otherwise mistakes will be made, and it is not always easy to trace the cause and location of errors. However, try to learn from your mistakes, and keep in mind that developing competence in computer usage is dependent upon the use you make of the computer.

## EXERCISES

10.1  Write a batch file, FORMSYS.BAT, which formats a disk in drive A, and copies the systems files on to it.

10.2  Write an AUTOEXEC.BAT file which does the following:

sets the prompt TIME TO ENTER DATA

sets a path to the Root Directory, to the WORDS directory, and to the LETTERS directory

sets the keyboard to the UK setting

activates the mouse

changes to the BATCH directory

lists all files in BATCH.

10.3  Modify the CONFIG.SYS file given in Chapter 10, so that the number of files which can be opened is 15, and the number of buffers, 5.

10.4  If a computer is dedicated to the use of WordStar (in the WORDS directory), write an AUTOEXEC.BAT file which starts WordStar as part of the boot-up process.

10.5  You have bought a piece of peripheral hardware which requires the driver file DISPLAY.SYS. What would you enter in the CONFIG.SYS file to set up the device driver?

# Appendix A
## Other Microcomputers

In Chapter 2, other types of microcomputers which could be used in a small business were mentioned. It was pointed out that the personal computer is by far the most popular microcomputer in the business world. There are, nevertheless, others which are suitable, but which have not so far gained the same foothold in data processing applications. In some cases, certain machines are regarded as particularly appropriate for other computer applications, but in most cases they have the same potential for data processing as the personal computer range.

The Apple Macintosh is an example of a machine which is viewed in this way. Many users see it essentially as a tool for desk-top publishing applications. While the various Macintosh models certainly have a formidable reputation in this area, they can also do anything a personal computer can do. But what makes a Mac different is that all its software packages have the same screen interface. The policy at Apple is that using a computer should be an intuitive process, and that there should be no need to learn anything about the operating system. This implies that users need little or no training, a major consideration which naturally has appeal to management. There is no doubt that the Apple designers are successful to a very great extent in putting their policy into practice, and it is interesting that the latest personal computer models are taking on board many of the Macintosh ideas on screen presentation and user interface.

The Macintosh interface is based on a screen which uses a combination of overlapping windows, icons (little diagrams), and pull-down menus to give access to applications. These are activated by a mouse which causes a pointer to move around the screen and allows the user to select an application by pressing a mouse button when the pointer targets on a window, icon or menu item. This is a very simplified description of the interface, but it does represent the basic idea. Keyboard input of text is entered as normal, so there is no difference from personal computer operations in that aspect of data processing activities. But one major advantage of the Macintosh is the quality of the screen display. It has a very high degree of clarity, and is a WYSIWYG presentation, showing both text and graphics as they are output on the printed page.

You may wonder why the Macintosh has not taken over the business data processing market. Many reasons are proposed, but what seems to be the most likely is that people like to stick with what they know, and most know the systems which run MS-DOS. Having learned to use application programs which run on MS-DOS, users do not necessarily find the Macintosh interface so intuitive, although many who use it, but who have never had a chance to learn to use MS-DOS efficiently, might well respond positively to the Mac.

Two other microcomputers which challenge the Macintosh in the area of *user-friendly* screen interface are the Atari ST and the Commodore Amiga. These are less expensive, and certainly can be used with success in the business world. The Atari ST has an excellent high-resolution monochrome display, and provides desk-top publishing at reasonable cost. The Amiga is a multi-tasking machine which also boasts high-resolution displays. In addition, its designers claim that it can emulate many other types of microcomputer, including MS-DOS machines.

The Acorn Archimedes is regarded by many as the most advanced of all microcomputers, and does provide some MS-DOS emulation. It can produce a screen resolution which few other microcomputers can rival, but it suffers at present from a paucity of software, particularly business software, when compared with other types of microcomputer.

Finally, there are the Amstrad PCW models, commonly referred to as 'word processors'. However, they are no less microcomputers than the others mentioned, and certainly, in terms of price, they offer a package which is extremely good value. Many small businesses get along perfectly well with PCWs, and do not feel the need to look elsewhere for their data processing needs.

# Appendix B
# Communications

Communications is one of the most exciting branches of information technology, and refers to the means by which computers can be linked to other computers. The connecting medium may be a cable or a telephone link, so that computer links can be anything from a metre to thousands of kilometres.

Linking computers in the same location by cable in a local area network is useful for centralising data processing without resorting to the expense of a mainframe or mini, and it is not necessary that all the computers linked together be of the same make or model. Furthermore, a network allows people to communicate with each other across computers. While this may not be too relevant where the computers are physically close, it is a valuable facility where links are of long distance. In this case, the communication occurs over telephone networks, for which appropriate hardware and software are required.

The hardware takes the form of a *modem* which is the link between telephone line and computer, and converts the computer's outgoing digital signals into the telephone line's analogue signals. A modem also converts incoming analogue signals into digital signals. There is a considerable range of modems on the market, as there are software packages. They are the programs which manage the communication, and the most useful facility they offer is to provide access to *E-mail* (electronic mail) systems.

An example provides an explanation of how E-mail works, and concerns the use of Telecom Gold. Say you, as a subscriber, wished to communicate with Roberta Bloggs, another subscriber. You call up the system with your modem and, when connected, you key-in your password to identify yourself (log-on), then key-in your message, addressing it to Ms Bloggs. When finished you disconnect (log-off). It is also possible to prepare your message before going on-line, saving it to disk and then sending it (sending a message this way obviously takes less time and therefore reduces time on-line, thus keeping down costs). Your message is stored on the Telecom Gold computer and is held there until Roberta logs-on, when she is told that there is a message for her.

The benefit you gain from using E-mail lies in a commitment to log-on regularly to check for incoming messages. Your correspondents must have the same commitment, of course, but assuming this to be so, E-mail is an extremely fast and efficient way of communicating with business associates. Telecom Gold is an international system so it can be used to contact subscribers abroad, but it is also possible to communicate with subscribers on other systems through *gateways*. One important point to bear in mind is that subscribers can access E-mail from any location where there is a computer, modem, software and telephone link available to them.

Other facilities available through communications are information services such as Prestel. Although they provide a vast amount of information about news, weather, travel, financial news, and so on, of particular interest are the specialist business information services. In addition Prestel provides an E-mail facility.

Another very useful and growing service provided by communications systems is *computer conferencing*. This is akin to E-mail, except that messages are public to all conference participants. This is a particularly useful way of co-operating to solve common problems.

These are just some of the services offered by communications. They are still in their infancy and are not yet being exploited by the business community, but the fact that many multi-national institutions have their own networks, which they use to co-ordinate their international activities, demonstrates the benefits of using these types of systems.

# Appendix C
# MS-DOS Version 4

The MS-DOS commands in this book are concerned with versions up to 3.3. This is no disadvantage for anyone who uses Version 4 because the syntax of the commands is the same, but the biggest differences between MS-DOS 4 and earlier versions, as far as you are concerned, is the *graphical shell* now provided, and the ability of Version 4.01 to use more than 32M on a hard disk (see Chapter 4 for information on earlier versions of MS-DOS in relation to hard disk size).

The graphical shell allows you to select commands from a series of menus rather than entering them at the keyboard. It does not, however dispense with the need to supply parameters, such as filenames, paths and disk drives; these are entered in *dialogue boxes*. Nevertheless, it does make this easier by backing the menus and dialogue windows with a *file system* screen which displays a current directory tree on the left and a current directory listing on the right. It is possible to *navigate* the file system to select files, etc, by highlighting as appropriate. The selected files, etc, are then entered in the dialogue box.

In spite of these differences, however, the user needs to understand how MS-DOS facilitates file management. The graphical shell does not in itself organise files any more than earlier versions of MS-DOS. It allows the users to adopt a more intuitive approach to working with MS-DOS, but there is no less a need for structure and planning which is informed by an understanding of MS-DOS.

# Appendix D
## Solutions to Exercises

Solutions which can be found in the text of the chapters are not repeated here, for example, all items in the Chapter 2 Exercises.

**Chapter 3**

3.1 Program : length of journey divided by fuel consumption
Data : 10 and 1,000.
3.3 There is not just one solution; the following is possible. Two files are required, one holds information about customers (name, address, etc, and model of car purchased), the other holds information about each of the ten models (model, servicing details, etc). The two files require a common field, possibly the name of the model, providing it is different from all other names (linked fields must contain unique information otherwise valid connections cannot be assured).

Creating one file only is incorrect. If all the information were put into one file, then details about the ten models is repeated many times, hence wasting both main memory and disk memory and slowing down database processing.

**Chapter 4**

4.4 **MD\DATAFILE**
4.5 As there are no files in DATAFILE, only the two lines with the full stops are listed.
4.6 **DIR/P**

**Chapter 5**

5.1 These can only be suggestions. What is important is that the

filenames are chosen with consistency and indicate the content of the files:
(i) JONES.LET (ii) HAMMRMAN.INV (iii) ANNUAL90.RPT (iv) MARKBURY.APL (v) TAX9091.DOC (vi) OIL1.RPT, OIL2.RPT, OIL3.RPT

## Chapter 6

6.2 All are internal except FORMAT

6.4 **DIR A:**

6.5 **DIR C:\WORDFILE\INVOICES**

6.6 **CD\WORDFILE\INVOICES**

6.7 (i) A\A1 (or \A\A1) (ii) \A\A1 (iii) A1 (or \A\A1) (iv) \A\A1 (v) \A\A1

## Chapter 7

7.1 (i) DISKCOPY, (ii) COPY, (iii) XCOPY or BACKUP, (iv) probably should not be backed-up, (v) DISKCOPY from master floppies, but after installation on a hard disk, XCOPY or COPY, (vi) COPY

7.2 **BACKUP *.LET A:/M/A    BACKUP *.LET B:/M/A**
(for twin floppy machines)

7.3 All files on the hard disk, modified or created since the last backup, would be backed-up, but the backup disk would be erased beforehand. To prevent erasure, include the /A option.

7.4 **BACKUP *.DOC A:/M/A    XCOPY *.DOC A:/M**
or
**BACKUP *.DOC B:/M/A    XCOPY *.DOC B:/M**
(for twin floppy machines)

7.5 **COPY\WORDFILE\LETTERS\*.LET A:**

7.6 **BACKUP *.INV A:    XCOPY *.INV A:**
or
**BACKUP *.INV B:    XCOPY *.INV B:**
(for twin floppy machines)

## Chapter 9

**Note:** There is more than one correct way of writing the batch files in the solutions to Exercises in this chapter.

9.1 **ECHO OFF**

**CLS**
**PROMPT Enter data here**
9.2 The errors in spelling result in the directory of WORDS being listed, rather than BATCH as was intended.

9.3 **ECHO OFF**                          **ECHO OFF**
    **CLS**                               **CLS**
    **CD\WORDS**                          **B:**
    **TYPE MYNAME.DOC**                   **CD\WORDS**
    **CD\**                               **TYPE MYNAME.DOC**
    **DIR**                               **CD\**
                                          **DIR**
                                          (for twin floppy machines)

9.4 **ECHO OFF**                          **ECHO OFF**
    **CLS**                               **CLS**
    **CD\UWORDFILE**                      **B:**
    **TYPE FRIEND1.DOC**                  **CD\WORDFILE**
    **PAUSE**                             **TYPE FRIEND1.DOC**
    **TYPE FRIEND2.DOC**                  **PAUSE**
                                          **TYPE FRIEND2.DOC**
                                          (for twin floppy machines)

9.5 **ECHO OFF**                          **ECHO OFF**
    **CLS**                               **CLS**
    **CD\WORDFILE**                       **B:**
    **COPY FRIEND*.DOC \WORDS**           **CD\WORDFILE**
    **DEL FRIEND*.DOC**                   **COPY FRIEND*.DOC \WORDS**
                                          **DEL FRIEND*.DOC**
                                          (for twin floppy machines)

9.6 **ECHO OFF**                          **ECHO OFF**
    **CLS**                               **CLS**
    **CD\**                               **B:**
    **MD NEW**                            **MD\NEW**
    **CD\NEW**                            **CD\NEW**
    **COPY\WORDS\FRIEND1.DOC**            **COPY\WORDS\FRIEND1.DOC**
    **TYPE FRIEND1.DOC**                  **TYPE FRIEND1.DOC**
                                          (for twin floppy machines)

**Chapter 10**

10.1 **ECHO OFF**
     **CLS**

      **XXFORMAT A:/S**
      **CD\BATCH**
      **DIR \*.BAT**

10.2  **ECHO OFF**
      **CLS**
      **PROMPT TIME TO ENTER DATA**
      **PATH C:\; C:\WORDS; C:\ WORDFILE\LETTERS**
      **KEYBUK**
      **MOUSE**
      **CD\BATCH**
      **DIR**

10.3  **FILES = 15**
      **BUFFERS = 5**
      (the remainder of CONFIG.SYS is unaltered)

10.4  **ECHO OFF**
      **CLS**
      **CD\WORDS**
      **WS**

10.5  **DEVICE = DISPLAY.SYS**

# Appendix E
# Further Reading

Barden R A, *How to Start in Office Information*, NCC Publications, 1988

Carter R, *Information Technology*, Pan Books, 1987

Elbra R A, *Guide to the Data Protection Act*, NCC Publications, 1984

Gosling P, *Easily into DOS*, Macmillan, 1989

Marlow A J, *Computerising Your Accounts*, NCC Blackwell, 1989

Megarry J, *Computers Mean Business*, Pan Books, 1984

Pritchard J A T, *Using an Electronic Mailbox*, NCC Publications, 1987

Simpson A, *The Best Book of DOS*, Howard W Sams, 1989

Wood M B, *Guidelines for Physical Computer Security*, NCC Publications, 1986

Wroe B, *Successful Computing in a Small Business*, NCC Publications, 1987

# Index